PRAISE FOR ANOTHER KIND OF COURAGE

Hollywood can't create real heroes, but God does! Doug Mazza and Steve Bundy are two of them. They're stronger than Thor, more powerful than Iron Man, and more trustworthy than Captain America. These dads are the real deal. Their strength to navigate the wilderness of disability is inspiring. With wisdom and tenacity, they are finding victory in the battle. I am grateful to be learning from them.

Kirk Cameron
Actor, Producer of Inspirational Films
and Co-Host of *The Way of the Master* Television Series

This book brings fathers face to face with what we have to deal with, but in a loving way. It allows you to be honest without the guilt of thinking that you don't love your child. You can't deal with anything that you don't bring into the light of day. *Another Kind of Courage* helps you face things you need to face.

Calvin Johnson
Sole Caregiver of Two Sons, One with Severe Autism

The most endangered species in America is not the spotted owl nor the snail darter, but the responsible father. More children will go to sleep tonight in a fatherless home than ever before in our nation's history.

James Merritt
Pastor, Author of *What God Wants Every Father to Know*
and Host of *Touching Lives* Television Program

Doug Mazza and Steve Bundy have written a powerful testament of authentic fathering in their new book, *Another Kind of Courage*. Even if you're not a special-needs father, I strongly encourage you to read this book. If God has entrusted you with raising a child with a disability, you need to know that other fathers struggle with the same issues you do. I was profoundly moved by the stories in this book—they made me a better father and a better man.

Rick Johnson
Bestselling Author of *Better Dads, Stronger Sons*
and *That's My Girl: How a Father's Love Empowers and Protects His Daughter*

Contents

Acknowledgements

This book has been a blessing to write—not only because God has had his thumb in our backs for six years but also because of the relationships represented in these pages. The courageous men who shared their stories with us have expanded our own vision of how awesome God is and how his infinite power works in each person's life regardless of the circumstances. These dedicated fathers, who never gave up on God's best for their families, truly humble us. We are honored to call them brothers in Christ.

We are grateful for a host of Joni and Friends Family Retreat directors and volunteers who minister to families affected by disability, providing much-needed respite and support. Only eternity will reveal the scope of your contribution. It has been our privilege to serve as retreat pastors and participate in discussion groups, where the unction for this book was born.

We would like to thank our dear friend Joni Eareckson Tada for her inspiration and the Joni and Friends board of directors for giving us an outstanding place to serve. As members of the leadership team, we have had the joy of serving alongside a talented and praying staff. As a result, we're even better fathers to our sons with disability. Keep up the great work.

Our sincere appreciation goes to senior editor Pat Verbal, whose contributions and skills have added so much to this book. She has been a steady force in helping us keep focused on writing in the midst of other responsibilities; without her, you would not be holding this book. Gratitude also goes to our literary agent and publisher Bill Denzel for his encouragement and to our gifted assistant editors Chris Ralston and Chonda Ralston. We also want to thank

Danelle Spatariu and Donna Rousseve for keeping us organized and moving forward.

Lastly, and most importantly, we praise our Lord and Savior Jesus Christ, who took on the form of an earthly man and walked the road of suffering to teach us how to live. He has never failed us in the darkest of nights and has been the light in our brightest days. He holds our children safely in his hands. Our prayer is that this book will inspire you to surrender to Jesus and discover another kind of courage—one rich in the promises of God.

Foreword

Before You Begin . . .

Not long ago, when my husband Ken was cleaning out our garage, he opened the kitchen door and held up a pair of Canadian crutches. "Do you want to dump these?" he asked. I glanced at them and got a lump in my throat. "Those are my Daddy's," I said softly. The aluminum was scraped and the rubber tips were scuffed, but the crutches brought into focus a flood of sweet memories.

Most memories harkened to the days my father would visit me when I was in the hospital recovering from a broken neck. With my life-altering injury, the Earecksons had suddenly become a special-needs family. It meant a complete change of family priorities and routines—and we were frightened. Facing a life of total and permanent paralysis, I was beginning to see how much I desperately needed Daddy.

Back then my father was in his seventies and had to use crutches because of his arthritis. I could always tell when he had arrived at the hospital and was coming to visit me—I could hear the heartwarming *click-click* of his crutches echoing up the hallway. *Oh boy, Daddy's here!* I would think, anticipating his visit. My father's presence meant more to me than I realized.

I was brand new to the world of disability, and it felt as though my life were spinning out of control; ripping apart at the seams; tearing apart into shreds. I wanted assurance—fatherly assurance—that somehow, some way everything was going to be *okay*. I remember my daddy picking me up when I was a little girl with a skinned knee and saying, "There, there, sweetheart, everything's going to be okay; Daddy's here." *This* is what my father's presence gave me.

When he held onto the guardrail of my hospital bed and smiled, I felt relieved; *Daddy's here. Everything's going to be okay.* It's what every child needs. Boys and girls with disabilities need a patriarchal figure who represents assurance. It's what dads do.

When a child is struggling with a disability—and his siblings are trying to deal with it too—a father becomes the symbol of stability and safety, of security and shelter. It's a tall order for any dad, and sadly, many are bowing out of the responsibility. For them a disability is simply too hard to face. Fathers today need guidance on how to develop "a long obedience in the same direction."[1] They need help creating that intangible sense of assurance every family needs.

It's why special-needs dads require a special kind of courage. I once heard a rabbi say that our natural human inclination is not toward courage but toward fear, timidity, and cowardice. However, when men demonstrate bravery in the face of overwhelming odds, it impacts *everyone* around them—including their family. When dads courageously step up to the plate of a non-stop, 24/7 disability routine and stick with it for the long haul, courage rises in the hearts of *all*. Especially their children.

Maybe you've seen the movie *Braveheart*—the scene before the Battle of Stirling Bridge, when the Scots start losing heart because of the size of the English army that shows up. Fear, self-doubt, and intimidation look to win before anybody even strikes a blow. Then Wallace and his band ride up from the rear on horseback, faces painted blue. Simply their act of showing up gives heart to the Scots, and they take the field and win the day. Special-needs dads need to know that when they "show up" and become that patriarchal figure who represents authority and assurance in the family, *it wins the day*.

The book you hold in your hands, *Another Kind of Courage*, describes the remarkable journeys of two special-needs dads who are helping their families win the day. These two men take us step by step through the challenges of everyday life with a disability while showing us how to bring stability and safety, security and shelter to the family. Let me briefly tell you about them.

Doug Mazza serves as president and COO of the Joni and Friends International Disability Center. Next to my own father, I know of no other dad who so tenderly and committedly cares for his family—especially his son Ryan, who has lived with Crouzon syndrome for over thirty-five years. Doug is *Braveheart* to Ryan—the kind of dad who constantly provides assurance that yes, with Jesus, everything will be okay.

Steve Bundy serves as vice president of our Christian Institute on Disability at our center. He and his wife, Melissa, parent two amazing boys: Jaron, who is typical, and Caleb, who has a chromosome deletion resulting in autism and other developmental disabilities. Raising Caleb is a joy, but a *huge* challenge. Caleb is no longer a little boy; he's a big, strapping teenager, and he keeps the Bundy family constantly on their toes.

These two men have my undying respect and admiration—I see their struggles, and I admire their valor. I wish every special-needs dad had the chance to sit long and talk much with Doug and Steve. And in a way, he can—*Another Kind of Courage* is an open book into the hearts of these men, revealing the kind of bravery that can help *any* dad win the day.

I pray that you will be blessed by the insights in this extraordinary book—and if *Another Kind of Courage* helps you to be a better parent to your own special-needs child, I encourage you to tell Doug and Steve. They'd be happy to hear from you, and you can always reach them through our website at www.joniandfriends.org/response.

Oh, and what did I do with those old crutches Ken found in our garage? Well, looking back on the way my own father influenced me—his daughter with a significant disability—there was no way they were heading for the trash bin. Those dusty, scarred crutches are hanging in our garage to this day, a constant reminder of the shelter, safety, and fatherly assurance my own daddy gave me in my greatest, my most desperate time of need.

And I hope that you are able to give the same to *your* child.

Joni Eareckson Tada
Joni and Friends International Disability Center
Spring 2014

Introduction

"Don't walk away!"

It's the heartfelt plea of countless wives around the world—wives whose husbands struggle with accepting a child with special needs. It's also the reason we wrote this book.

Real men don't walk away—physically, emotionally, or spiritually. Real men seek ways to come to grips with their roles and responsibilities as husbands and fathers, even when the journey is not what they expected. Real men learn to live with *another kind of courage*.

We know this journey. As fathers of sons with disabilities, we both have traveled the well-worn path of the unknown and unexpected. We've walked where fears hide in dark places, nearly paralyzing us. We've also navigated the difficult course you find yourself on—the one that caused you to open this book.

We are the first to admit that we have not always made the best decisions. At times we've failed as husbands and fathers. Yet God's love and grace have been utterly sufficient, and with his help we've also made some wise choices for our families. So we submit the following to you with a great sense of humility and with the hope that on these pages you will find the help you need.

Another Kind of Courage can be your companion and guide. It is filled with insights from men whose stories offer encouragement, strength, and hope—even humor. Laughter is like a refreshing stream encountered while walking along life's dry and dusty trail. It gives us a moment to stop, rest, and refocus on life's God-given treasures.

The good news is, you're not alone! This uphill climb of coping with disabilities is filled with men who have gone before you and are still climbing higher. They will point out to you where the loose rocks wait, and they stand ready to help you tie another knot in the end of your frayed rope.

How can a father embrace his own brokenness before embracing his child's? How can a man keep his marriage a priority in the midst of emotional turmoil? What does it mean to be the leader of the family when one's internal compass does not point to true north?

How does a man stay—when he feels like walking away?

Whether you are a first-time dad or have been parenting for years, *Another Kind of Courage* can help you become a better husband and father.

Doug Mazza and Steve Bundy

CHAPTER 1

Courage When There Are No Answers

BY STEVE BUNDY

God enters by a private door into every individual.
RALPH WALDO EMERSON

Few things shake a man to the core of his being like hearing that his son or daughter has been diagnosed with a disability. Some men receive this news in a delivery room or doctor's office, others in the chaos of an emergency room. Still others hear words like "your child is not typical" during a parent-teacher conference at school and walk back to the car in shock, clutching pamphlets on special education services.

No matter where it's received such news hits hard. Even men of strong conviction and integrity can easily lose their way and become plagued by anger, fear, and depression. These fathers may question what they thought to be true about life. And men of faith may question how a loving God, who promised to never give anyone more than they are able to bear,[1] could allow such a circumstance

17

into their lives. The news hits every man differently but most experience a similar grief, similar pain, and find themselves suddenly with similar needs.

Nothing Prepares You

Dave Deuel, academic director of The Master's Academy International, had already experienced the joy of fatherhood with the birth of his first child. He and his wife Nancy were in the process of buying their first home as they prepared for baby number two. However, things didn't go as planned.

> No one could have prepared me for the news. I had successfully finished school, gotten married, taken my first teaching job, and moved from one coast to another. Nancy and I were expecting our second child and anticipating a typical birth. When the moment of delivery arrived, the physician was hyper-vigilant. I remember wondering why he didn't lighten up a little. After all, births were supposed to be joyful occasions. But as our little girl entered the world, we began to realize this wasn't a typical birth. Our baby hardly made a sound. The look of panic on the nurses' faces and the deafening hush in the room sent a sick feeling to my stomach. When I eventually was allowed to hold our daughter, her skin was ash-blue, her tiny body limp and motionless. I watched as my wife slept peacefully, unaware of the growing reality that something was very wrong. That night I remember driving home numb, exhausted, and scared.

A growing number of fathers can relate to Dave's experience. The rate of children born with special needs is skyrocketing. The Centers for Disease Control reports that one in every 88 children born today in the U.S. will have some form of autism. Thirteen percent of children ages 13-17 have developmental disabilities which can impair their learning, communication, and physical skills and abilities.[2]

Rick Copus, a worship leader and the founder of the Rick Copus Band, understands what fathers of these children will face.

> I never planned on being a father at the young age of twenty-two. I was foolish and self-centered, with grand hopes for the future. But the night our first child was born with a disability, my life changed forever. And to make matters worse, as little Autumn lay in the hospital's neonatal intensive care unit in a fragile state, our house was being burglarized. I couldn't believe it. I returned home to find that thieves had ransacked our belongings and taken many of our most valued possessions. It suddenly hit me hard that nothing I dreamed about for my life was going to come true. In the early months, I just did my best to care for my wife and daughter, keep my job and hold my emotions together so no one would detect how frightened I really was. Soon Autumn began having grand mal seizures, and the hospital became our second home. Our lives turned into a continuous roller coaster ride.

Who will stand beside men like Dave and Rick to assure them that even in their darkest hour God is still there? Too often, family and friends don't know what to say, and their looks of pity make parents of children with disabilities want to hide. When courage seems lost, these fathers need a friend who can open their eyes to the sovereignty of God's grace and his power to transform even the most difficult circumstances into times we can celebrate God's goodness and experience his joy.

For over a decade, I've been called to stand in that place—not only as a pastor and disability ministry leader, but as the father to a son with multiple severe disabilities. Like Dave and Rick and every other father of a child with a disability, I have asked the same gnawing questions that steal a man's sleep. In my desperation, I've wrestled with God as Isaac's son Jacob did and begged God not to let me go until he had changed me.[3]

If this is your story as well—if you are a father wrestling with these difficult issues—you need to know that you are not alone. In this book, you'll meet other fathers who have faced the very things you are facing today and are here to stand with you. Our desire is to offer you a reason for the hope that we have found in Christ Jesus, for our children and our own lives.

I am certain that you have many questions. And while we don't claim to have all of the answers, we acknowledge that no question is insignificant. That includes the question I fielded one Sunday morning from one of my youngest inquirers—my son, Jaron.

Daddy, How Big Is God?

It was just the two of us that morning, me behind the wheel and my four-year-old son Jaron in his seat, staring at the scenery as we drove to church. Most Sundays there were four, but that day Caleb, our older son, was ill and my wife, Melissa, kept him at home. I might have joined them had I not previously committed to help in our church's disability ministry. So it was just Jaron and me cruising to church.

Like most children, Jaron had the uncanny ability to ask simple questions with enormous implications. That day he simply asked, "Daddy, how big is God?"

Wow! What a question from a child who had yet to spend a day in kindergarten! A sense of pride ran through me. I felt delighted that Jaron had God on his mind. Maybe I was doing something right as his father.

In graduate school, I had picked up a skill that served me well. When uncertain as to how to answer, or when time is needed to think, I answer a question with a question. Since Jaron had caught me off guard, I resorted to this technique.

"How big do *you* think God is, son?"

Jaron did the natural thing for a child trying to comprehend the "bigness" of God. He looked for something he could use as a comparison. Through the window, he could see the rugged San Gabriel Mountain range a short distance away. They were a familiar sight, green in the spring and blanketed in snow during the winter. Mount San Gorgonio rises to a height of 11,500 feet. "Is God bigger than the mountains?" he asked.

"Yes, Jaron," I said, "God is bigger than the mountains. In fact, he *created* the mountains." I reminded him of the creation story he had heard in Sunday school and conjured up as many word pictures as I could to help his young mind grasp the difficult concept.

"How big is God?" It's a simple question with a complex answer. It's also a question asked by fathers of children with special needs—fathers like you and me. Like Jaron we often compare God to the biggest visual we can find. Our minds are drawn to the apparently devastating life circumstances of our children. The questions buzz in our heads: *If this God is so big, can't he fix every disability?* Better yet, *Why doesn't he prevent them in the first place?*

Is God really a mighty fortress to be reckoned with, or just a crutch for old ladies to lean on? Where is this God of all the earth who through his spoken word called all creation into existence?

I have asked those questions over and over again. They have come to me in the darkness as I lie in bed, in the daylight as I go about my work, and in the artificial light of hospital hallways where I've paced for hours. They take up residence in my mind just like they do in yours. You've probably learned, as I have, that while questions are plentiful, sometimes answers seem few and much too elusive.

My Story

My son Caleb was born with a partial chromosome deletion, and I have to admit that my view of God changed and was even shattered the moment I heard the news. Like fathers everywhere, I had high expectations for my son. I had looked forward to the small things in fatherhood that make life grand: first words, first steps, first game of catch, first day of school. My mind had often fast-forwarded to my boy's graduation, his first car, even to the day of his wedding.

That was before I heard the words "partial chromosome deletion." The more the doctors explained medical terms, the more my world felt like it was unraveling. We men can endure anything but helplessness. It's not part of our wiring. We want to fix things and make our family's world right and safe and joyful. What the doctors told me took away all those opportunities. There would be no fishing trips, no learning to bat a ball, no sprinting for a touchdown. There would be no teaching my son about life by passing down my years of experience. For Caleb there would be endless disability. The prognosis dissolved my dreams and hopes for him as I had understood them. And that wasn't the end of it. Caleb's disabilities would later include severe global delay, low muscle tone (hypotonia), autism, and a string of other medical complications.

Interestingly, before Caleb's birth I worked with adults with developmental disabilities while I attended seminary. My wife and I had dedicated our lives to world missions and had already spent some time on the mission field, where many of the people we worked with had disabilities. Looking back, I wonder if this was divine symmetry preparing us for the life we would lead with Caleb. On the other hand, we belonged to a denomination that held the belief that children like Caleb were not born to believers like us. It seems silly to say now, but many religious people continue to believe this to be true.

To understand what a difficult transition it was for me to become the father of a child with special needs, let me emphasize that the news about Caleb's condition completely contradicted what I believed at the time. My world seemed to sway and tremble as I tried to reconcile how God could allow such a thing to happen to someone like me, a faithful follower. Most of our friends believed the same things we did, so consequently, they were ill-equipped to give us the comfort and ministry we needed, right when we needed it most. Truthfully, I hardly knew how to comfort myself. Well-intended friends let us know that they were praying for Caleb's immediate healing and would stand with us for increased faith. Some even counseled us that we had to resist the devil because he had stolen my son's health, and we had to reclaim it from him. And there was the constant encouragement to confess and claim healing for our son lest we "confess a negative report" and cause our son to remain like this for the rest of his life. I believe we and these friends were zealous and sincere in our pursuit of God's best, but suddenly my family's situation did not match my beliefs. I found myself forced off the predictable path I had so confidently followed.

The Problem with Men

There was another problem: I am a man. There are a few things no man can stand, and heading the list is being told he is lost. How many times have husbands and wives had the same old argument, with the man refusing to ask for directions? *Don't tell me how to get there, I can figure it out. Whoever put up these stupid road signs must have been on drugs. Leave me alone! I'm not lost, and I don't need help.*

But I *was* lost. Emotionally lost. Spiritually adrift. There were days when the man in the mirror appeared as a stranger with only a vague resemblance to me.

Loss of control paralyzed me, as it does most men. We want to be in control of everything. It's why we love the television remote control. Just a click of a button and presto, I control the world of TV with hundreds of channels at my beck and call. We men need it. It's what makes us strong, driven, and ambitious—or so we think. A child's disability strips all control from our hands.

It can also attack one's manhood. Say the word "manly" to most men and images of Russell Crowe in *Gladiator* or Mel Gibson in *Braveheart* come to mind. For most men, words like "manhood" and "weakness" don't even belong in the same sentence. It's like a javelin to the heart of our male ego to have a child with disabilities because there's nothing we can do about it. In those early days, doubt crowded my mind. *What kind of a man am I? How could such a weak offspring come from me? What went wrong with my sperm?* Men who have children without special needs have a hard time understanding how difficult it can be to reconcile your manhood with the apparent weakness of the child before you.

Greg Schell, director of the Washington State Fathers Network and the father of a 33-year-old daughter with Down syndrome, believes the issue is that men are socialized in a very different way than women, which often leaves them less prepared to handle a child's disability. "Men learn from an early age that they must be tough when the chips are down. They're encouraged to 'suck it up' and to fix any problem that comes their way. But when they learn they have a child with special needs, they face a dilemma when they realize that even the smartest minds in the world can't change this new reality."[4]

These hurting men are yearning deep inside for someone to tell them that they did nothing wrong. When Caleb was born, I longed to hear the affirmation, "You did **not** do anything **wrong**!" But those words did not come until much later.

Reality Is Not an Option

When my friend John received the news that his unborn daughter would likely not survive past twenty-five weeks in the womb, he was forced to face a grim reality. The only two options the doctors offered were to allow the child to die in the womb or to perform a C-section, which his daughter might not survive. If she did survive, she would most likely be profoundly disabled.

As John grappled with the weight of this decision, he and I prayed together, shared truths from God's Word, and cried. Afterwards, John asked me to write down some of our discussion. Here is an excerpt from the letter I sent him:

February 4, 2007

John,

I want to thank you for sharing your raw feelings with me, which is never easy, and let you know that your feelings are completely normal and natural. Although I don't exactly know what you're going through, my journey has been fueled with similar challenges and I relate to your fears and concerns.

First, let me say that your daughter is very well cared for and loved by God, as are you and Julie. Regardless of the dire scenarios you have been given and of those running through your mind about the life of your daughter, remember she is precious in the sight of the Lord.

At the risk of sounding overly spiritual, I encourage you to really ponder this thought. It may be the one thought that gets you through some difficult times: God loves and cares for your family! God is in control in your out-of-control circumstances. He will meet you at your point of need and provide the grace you need to be the

25

husband and father you long to be. He has not abandoned you, nor punished you for some known or unknown sin. It doesn't seem like it now, but your family's future is bright and promising! God called you. God gave you Julie as your wife, and God gave you your daughter. Blessed be the name of the Lord.

Unfortunately, bad things happen in life, and it sucks! No one can ever answer the "why my child?" question. Because of the fall of Man (so I believe), things go wrong—sometimes very wrong. And God allows suffering, but we must choose how we will respond. You, my friend, may walk through this fire, but you will not travel alone.

Wow! That sounds so religious! You're probably thinking, "What garbage! Where is God in this? I just want a healthy daughter." I do understand!

Yet I wish someone had come alongside of me when Caleb was born to reassure me of who I was as a man, a disciple of Christ, a husband, father, and leader—to say that it was going to be all right and that God was still pleased with me. No one did, and you know my journey.

Your daughter may be perfectly fine, and Julie may carry her long enough for a healthy delivery! This is my prayer for you! But the prognosis at this time is not favorable, and I am not going to sugarcoat anything. Life for parents of children with special needs is difficult; for some more than others.

I can't deny that not a day goes by that I do not wish Caleb were "normal." And some days I feel tremendous anger at God for Caleb's condition. That's right—anger. Some days my anger is really about myself and my pride. To say that having a child with a disability is inconvenient is an understatement—it is consuming in every possible way.

I must also admit, however, that no day goes by that I don't thank God for Caleb. I love him with a deep passion and his life has taught me more about living, laughing, crying, suffering, sin, and victory than any other person I've ever met. And every night I say a prayer over Caleb. I watch him sleeping in his bed and remind myself that God's love and grace are greater than I can ever imagine and the mystery of life and death are beyond my grasp. I am utterly and fully dependent on God.

We don't need to discuss the sanctity of life, human dignity, purpose, and the meaning of life. Intuitively, you know your daughter needs a father who will fight for her to the end; one who believes her life is as valuable as any other, regardless of her disabilities and limitations. I'm sure you struggle to justify having an immediate C-section with the understanding that the baby will likely not survive and go home to her Heavenly Father. You may think this would be better for her than living with the disabilities. Chances are your next child will be healthy, right? But it's not so easy.

Your daughter is actually God's daughter. She is God's first and yours second. She is in his image first and yours second. Let that sink in. Everything you believe in and have stood for will be tested by the circumstance before you. Your daughter may be born with severe disabilities that will forever change your future, forever alter your view of what it means to have a family, take vacations, go for a walk, pay for ballet lessons, and all the stuff you dream for her. This can turn you upside down and inside out. Not only will you have to face the great disappointment of not receiving the child you expected, but you must face the challenges of her disabilities.

27

So, I write with no pretentious illusions. I offer no, "Oh, what a blessing from God. His grace will be sufficient. God chose you because he knew you were the right couple for a special needs child." Well-meaning people with no understanding of disabilities don't know how ridiculous that sounds to parents struggling to cope with their child's diagnosis.

Still, we have many good days and joyful times with Caleb. Our family has developed deep, intimate relationships because of our journey with him. Melissa and I look at life and the world completely differently than before. Despite our shortcomings, we feel closer to God and to one another. Our ministry to others is deeper. We've suffered and can empathize with people in a greater way. God uses our brokenness, and I wouldn't change this.

The way forward on this difficult journey is always uphill, but it's still forward. I love you, my friend, and am here for you! I'm praying for you.

Steve

John and Julie made the decision to have their baby delivered by C-section, giving their daughter her only chance for survival. The following days were filled with exhausting medical decisions and heart-wrenching choices made with no idea what the outcome might be—all done in an effort to give their daughter a future and a hope. Four days after her birth, their daughter went home to be with the Lord.

It is during such times that the real questions begin, that a man's world seems to go upside down, that a man realizes what minimal control he has over life—his or that of his family. But it is also a priceless opportunity to see life, and ourselves, in a truer light.

What Is True Manhood?

In the book of Philippians, the apostle Paul talks about the change that Christ brought in his life of self-confidence and self-righteousness. Before knowing Christ, Paul placed his confidence solely in his abilities, his education, his strength; he felt in control of his world. However, as he experienced suffering and brokenness, Paul discovered that his manhood was not based in his strengths, but rather in his weaknesses that were made strong through faith.

True manhood looks nothing like the strong, self-capable men displayed in Hollywood movies or men's magazines. When it comes to pulling your world back together, there is no "four-step" formula. As Christian men, our manhood must take on a new image that moves from self-confidence and personal success to complete dependence upon God.

Men are compartmental thinkers. We like each area of our lives tucked in its place, easy to find, easy to use. This allows us to deal with one thing at a time instead of being overwhelmed by life's many parts. Sensory overload occurs when we mix up the various compartments. For example, when I watch television, I'm in my mental "TV compartment." That's my TV room, and I like it to stay that way. I don't like to watch TV, play with my kids, and talk on the phone at the same time. Women don't always understand this. It frustrates my wife when I don't turn my head to talk while I watch television. Women don't understand that many men are incapable of being in the "TV compartment" and in the "talking to my wife with full attention compartment" at the same time. Because we men can't do both at the same time, something suffers—and unfortunately, it's usually the wife.

Likewise, we often create a compartment for God. We think we have him pretty well figured out. That is until life becomes messy and our compartments begin to collapse into each other. God, as we thought we knew him, no longer fits our expectations. He has left his box. In fact, not only has he left his box but God has spilled over into all the other compartments of our lives. We no longer control him or how and when he intervenes in our lives.

Remember Jaron's question . . . How big is God? The answer: Much bigger than we can imagine!

While we tend to focus on what God is *not* doing for us and our child, God *is* at work protecting and keeping our lives in his care. He constantly demonstrates his grace to us even when we shake our fist and demand an explanation for our child's lot in life. He prepares others to comfort us while we run and hide, sometimes resorting to harmful vices like pornography, alcohol, or sex to try to ease our pain. God stands ready to restore us to a right relationship with him even though we feel like turning our backs on him.

God doesn't belong in a box. Instead, we need to allow him free rein to help us navigate the challenging waters of our child's disability.

Looking with God's Perspective

Your child is no accident. God is not sitting on the edge of his throne biting his fingernails hoping that everything will be all right. The struggles, challenges, hardships, and pain you and your family experience are not beyond God's control. He knew your child before he or she was formed in the womb.[5] Scripture says all things, including people, were created by and for God.[6] God created man in his image, which speaks of each individual's inherent worth and dignity regardless of abilities or functions—the things we usually focus on. A fellow-struggler in the Old Testament named Job said of God: "You clothed me with skin and flesh, and knit me together with bones and sinews. You have granted me life and steadfast love, and your care has preserved my spirit" (Job 10:11-12, *NRSV*).

Our society usually focuses on the physical. We celebrate athletes and beautiful people. When we meet someone, our first judgment is based on appearance. But people are so much more than their physical veneer. Every individual has a spiritual component called a soul. The body ages, grows weak, is subject to disease, and ultimately dies. No one leaves this life alive—at least not physically. The soul, however, lives forever. The apostle John wrote a letter to his friend in a distant church saying, "Dear friend, I pray that you may enjoy good health and that all may go well with you, even as your soul is getting along well" (3 John 2).

Did you catch that? He prays for the person's body *and* soul.

Children with disabilities have souls that are as vibrant and alive as any person without a disability. Your child, no matter his or her special need, has a soul that cannot be damaged by missing or misaligned chromosomes.

God's Gift of Emotions

King David of the Bible has always captivated me. Here is a man who experienced just about every emotion one can imagine. Fortunately for us, those emotions were written down in the Old Testament book of Psalms for the world to see. David freely expressed his hatred, love, greed, lust, sorrow, joy, confusion, and faith. Though most men won't admit it, we are emotional creatures. We just don't show it because we've learned to press down worry, dilute fear, and ignore all the emotions we don't like. Disability changes that. Disability teaches us, even forces us, to experience and express the full range of human emotion, like David did.

Many of us think emotional displays (other than anger) are weaknesses reserved for women. Let's be clear—this idea is nonsense. All humans are emotional beings. Sure, we express our emotions differently than women, but they are there and just as real.

No doubt you've ridden the roller coaster of emotion—hopeful one moment, utterly despairing the next; confident one day, ready to give up the next. Your feelings are normal. You are not alone!

You have a right to be emotional when there are no answers for your child's special needs. But you don't have a right to give up. *Elohim,* **God Our Father,** is present in every situation you face. He is all-knowing and all-powerful even when you can't understand his purposes. David reminds us of this in Psalm 46: "God is our refuge and strength, an ever-present help in trouble. Therefore we will not fear, though the earth give way and the mountains fall into the heart of the sea . . . The Lord Almighty is with us."[7]

The Bible is the well I go to when my emotions begin to overwhelm me. God's promises refresh and support us in difficult times. For example, 1 Peter 5:7 says, "Cast all your anxiety on him because he cares for you." This verse says we can toss off our anxiety. Imagine the powerful spin of an Olympic athlete as he hurls a 17-pound shot put more than 70 feet into the air. What a thought! We are told to take our worries and throw them on God. He doesn't mind. He actually invites it.

That verse also reminds me that I am not alone. I am not casting my care to the wind or writing it on a sticky note for later. Instead, I am casting it upon God. He can handle it. He's got big shoulders. If I leave it with him, I know it will be taken care of—even if the outcome is not what I expected.

Finally this verse assures me that God cares for me *and* my child. This promise is not just for me, but also for those under my covering who cannot speak for themselves. No problem is too small for God to notice or too big for him to handle. God cares for my family. That gives me great peace and confidence.

There is no shame in facing our emotions. The mighty warrior king David wept. Jesus wept—several times.[8] Do we think we're stronger or manlier than David or Jesus? There is no shame in expressing our emotions. While it's true that much of the burden of strength in a family falls to fathers, dealing with the pain we feel doesn't prevent us from being the steel our families need.

God's Grip Holds

When disability strikes and questions mount, we feel a loss of control. But our loss of control can be a blessing in disguise. The truth is that we were never really in control in the first place. None of us can control whom God places in our families, or what the future will look like, or the emotions we'll feel. Man certainly has never controlled God. Thinking we are in control of our own lives is just an illusion and having a child with a disability destroys that fantasy. In reality, true contentment only comes when our illusions of control are replaced with this truth: *God is never more in control than when we feel out of control.*

Dave and Rick, who you met earlier in this chapter, had much to learn about giving God control of their lives and families. As they did, the Light[9] began to dispel their darkness.

Dave Deuel

The day after Joanna's birth, the doctors said, "Things are bad. She may not live. If she does, she may have brain damage." My legs buckled and my mind cried out, 'Lord, where are you?' After waiting two weeks, the chromosome tests were thrown out due to contamination. We didn't want to put our little girl through testing again. My heart ached, but familiar verses wandered into my thoughts . . . Children are a gift from the Lord[10]. . . Take delight in the Lord, and he will give you the desires of your heart.[11] What I desired was a healthy and normal baby. These verses were not working for me. The confusion was overwhelming. In the darkness, life seemed to be over.

But life was not over. I know now that a bright new day had dawned for my entire family, although it would take a while for us to fully recognize and accept it. God's grace would soon ease the pain and lift the darkness in ways we couldn't have dreamed of at that time.

Rick Copus
The first five years of Autumn's life were filled with medical challenges. The exhaustion and stress led to several job losses and even a divorce. As a single dad of a child with cerebral palsy and quadriplegia, my loneliness was incomprehensible. I turned to drugs and alcohol to cope, but soon realized I was living on the edge and needed to change. In my daughter's smile, I knew God was there. I thank him for giving me the ability to focus under pressure and to eventually turn to a spiritual fellowship. There I gave my life to Christ as my Lord and Savior. That's when everything in my life and my family began to change for the better. Autumn never let her physical condition get her down and her perseverance taught me to keep going even when it seemed impossible. In my new life I met a wonderful woman who joined me in living a life affected by disabilities. God has forgiven much in my life and redeemed me for his purpose.

God Is Big Enough

Just as my son Jaron pondered how big God is, you probably have as well. I've discovered that God is big enough to know our needs, feel our hurts, understand our disappointments, sense our fears, notice our mood swings, sympathize with our concerns, and empathize with our pains.

You've been through the wringer, my friend. You've been pressed, crushed, and kicked around by circumstance. Most likely, you've blamed yourself for events you couldn't control. But in it all, know that you are not alone. There are many of us in the "Brotherhood of Wounded Fathers." I didn't start the fraternity—I didn't even choose to join it. Neither did you, but here we are, members nevertheless. It helps to know that there are others like us. It's comforting to realize that others understand my pain—your pain. The one thing that makes the most difference in my daily life is to believe that God is big enough to overcome any problem my family might face.

You may look at your child and say, "It's unfair." But God never promised that life would meet our standards of fairness, only that he would be there in the middle of our crisis when we humbly come to him. He is the Answer when there are no answers. And his grace does not fail.

> " . . . as a father deals with his own children, encouraging, comforting and urging you to live lives worthy of God . . ."
> 1 THESSALONIANS 2:11-12

GROWTH STEPS

1. God is not surprised by disabilities. It is okay to ask God the hard questions.

   What is your question for God today?

2. In times of crises, God has something important to say to you.

   What has God said to you today through this chapter?

3. *Elohim*—God My Father is all-powerful, all-knowing, and is present with me in every situation.

   Read Deuteronomy 6:4-5 and use it as your daily prayer.

CHAPTER 2

Courage When Life Spins Out of Control

BY DOUG MAZZA

Christ is a substitute for everything,
but nothing is a substitute for Christ.

H.A. IRONSIDES

The onset of a child's disability can feel like a heavy fog that engulfs your family and gets thicker with each passing day. Have you ever driven through a "blinding fog"? It is literally impossible to see even a couple of feet ahead of your vehicle. You inch along trying to make progress, straining to be ready for the next turn, yet feeling a sense of fear and trepidation because you have no idea what lies ahead. It's scary and exhausting . . . much like those first days of my son's life.

This can't be happening—not to my child! I won't let it!

The seemingly endless days of medical tests and the sleepless nights spent researching words you can't even pronounce eventually take their toll. Soon you can't eat, work, sleep, or even pray.

And the pressure is compounded when you look at your wife who is also falling apart, as you stand by feeling powerless to help. As a man you know how it is; if we can't fix something, we tend to start blaming ourselves. And that only adds to the anxiety.

Perhaps your family's days of medical diagnoses and waiting rooms are just beginning. Whether a child's disability is intellectual or physical, from birth or the result of a tragic accident, I've found that the first days are remarkably similar for most families. While I can't lift the fog for you, in this chapter I can point you to the only One who knows the way through.

The Dreaded Waiting Room

Brent Olstad is a music composer/publisher and Area Director of Joni and Friends in Southern Oregon. He grew up with a stronger-than-usual distaste for waiting rooms. For him, a waiting room always seemed like a prelude to bad news—like when the dentist says you need a root canal or the auto mechanic tells you your transmission is shot . . . and neither one is covered by insurance! Brent's aversion to waiting rooms grew stronger when his oldest son Bryce was diagnosed with spina bifida, hydrocephalus, and other complications.

> I remember how uncomfortable it felt to sit in a waiting room filled with strangers, hiding behind outdated magazines. Sometimes I would wonder what circumstances had brought them there, but mostly I fixated on my own problems. Names were called by the nurses whose voices sounded cold and sterile. I knew that each person who walked through those doors had needs, but I didn't have the emotional strength to care, so I just waited.
>
> As time went on I found myself in other waiting rooms wondering if my son would live or die. I sat in straight-backed chairs,

drinking old coffee from paper cups, and watching TV ads that claimed life would be great if I used a certain brand of toothpaste. Time seemed to stand still in those rooms waiting for answers to countless questions.

In waiting rooms, I also had ample time to scrutinize each moment of my life as I tried to create a sense of reason behind what was happening. I knew the error of my ways and the rewards of my efforts. I questioned the balance in life—the balance between sorrow and happiness, pain and joy, cause and effect. I thought about my son's pain, and how I might have caused it.

Brent's profound sense of helplessness became an inward journey of wrestling with himself to try to regain the equilibrium he once took for granted.

A Sense of Failure

For some fathers of children with special needs loss of control also brings bouts of regret, guilt, and shame. This was true for Jon Ebersole, director of U.S. Area Ministries at Joni and Friends. Jon recalls how this sense of heaviness struck him one day after trying to teach his teenage daughter Jessica how to drive.

I collapsed onto my bed feeling like a failure as a father—again. I had become impatient with my daughter during her driving practice. This sense of disappointment in myself had become commonplace. In my head I understood that both of my twin daughters had cerebral palsy resulting from their premature births. I understood the impact it had on their abilities, yet I found myself irritated and impatient time and again. In my heart I agonized over this as a father and as a follower of Jesus. I was perplexed by why God wasn't changing me when I had asked him

DOUG MAZZA AND STEVE BUNDY

to do so many times. The Bible makes it clear that God wants every parent to be kind and loving and to always be their child's greatest encourager. I consistently felt discouraged and my situation seemed hopeless.

I began to realize that I had a disdain for weakness—in myself and in others. Throughout high school and college I was at the top of my class. I knew God was real and believed that my job was to perform to my highest ability in everything I did. I saw times of sickness as a nuisance to be endured and pushed through as much as possible. Growing older I came to realize that I was more driven than most and this contributed to feelings of discontentment. I was hard on myself, always focusing on conquering the next task. I came to see that these traits were the catalyst for my lack of patience with my daughters' disabilities. And while I knew my attitude and self-focus were wrong, I couldn't seem to change. Somehow I had gotten stuck.

My Fast-Track to a Brick Wall

As the president and chief operating officer at Joni and Friends, I have worked alongside Brent and Jon. These men are Christian brothers and leaders whom I admire and respect. But more importantly, as the father of a son with profound physical and intellectual disabilities, I understand their struggles. I, too, was a driven young man, much like Jon. I graduated from a private college, ready to embark on whatever adventure life had for me. I immediately received a letter from the President of the United States, inviting me to join the United States Army along with 30,000 other guys that month—that's what a college education would get you in 1969. Looking back now I wouldn't have missed that opportunity for anything. There is no greater place to become trained in the reality of "cause and effect" than in the U.S. Army. Sergeants bark commands, and without question the recruits answer, "Yes, Drill Sergeant!" Talk about control, discipline, balance, and direction. The military does a fine job of preparing America's soldiers—for which we are deeply grateful. While all of the lessons the military teaches are helpful in life, no one can prepare you for the messiness of family life and fatherhood, especially when your child has profound disabilities.

After the Army, I started my business career. While I had always believed in God and that Jesus was his Son, I had no actual concept of a personal relationship with God. I believed that God was out there, somewhere, surrounding the world, doing whatever it was that God did. When I felt pressured or in trouble, I often prayed long enough to give him my list of needs. I cringe now thinking how my written prayers back then were more like a negotiation than a thankful communication with the Maker of the Universe. These seasons of prayer were followed with my own plans for my life with me in control once again as the author of my destiny. What made it even worse is that my life in general was pretty good. My system seemed to work, and I benefited from what the world called success.

Before the age of 40, I was an executive in a major multinational corporation. I had already been to Harvard to discuss our business plan, and eventually became the senior American executive. Numerous departments that required a myriad of skills reported to me—from advertising to production planning and many others. I also quickly discovered that each day I went to work I faced huge decisions that could end my career. We coined the phrase, "CEO actually stands for a Career Ending Opportunity." I thrived on embracing new challenges, and life hummed along pretty well. However, I soon discovered a disturbing asterisk to my theory of control. Along my way to the top, God gave me a son whose birth was a complete game-changer.

Ryan was born with severe facial and skull deformities caused by a rare chromosome condition. The medical specialists explained to us that early in the development of the fetus the sutures (or soft spots) are fused together in the skull. At that time, very few babies with this condition, called Crouzon syndrome, were born alive. God must have had his hand on Ryan because he kept one suture in the skull open in his forehead, allowing his brain to grow to its full size albeit severely advanced in front of his face. The brain pushed his eyes out of their sockets and dislocated his upper jaw. Ryan's upper respiratory system was also affected, and his thumbs and toes were twisted by another defect. Ryan was only expected to live for a few brief moments.

When he made it to two weeks of age, the doctors decided to try an experimental operation. Ryan was transferred to Children's Hospital in Chicago and underwent his first craniofacial advancement surgery. The doctors cut Ryan's skull from its base to the tip of the nose, and from ear to ear. They laid his head open and removed all the bone from around his skull. The *dura* muscle was used to ease the brain back into the bowl of the skull and the surgeons began replacing bone around Ryan's head to give him the shape of a normal skull. His eyes were still pressed severely forward, and he still had respiratory problems. It was the first of thirteen operations that Ryan would undergo over three years, in an attempt to save his life.

During all of these procedures Ryan developed many complications and side effects. He rejected his own bone and an infection led the surgeons to remove the bone in his forehead. Lacking the protection that his forehead provided his brain, Ryan needed something to give him the likeness of a "normal" face. In another operation, Ryan's ribs were transplanted from his chest to his head, forming a frame above the eyebrow that was literally wired together.

Our family spent many emotionally-charged hours in intensive care rooms, hospital hallways and quiet dark places, looking for answers to all the standard questions: *How did this happen?*

41

What should we do next? And the big one . . . *Why?* The more I applied my standard procedures of analysis, the less things made sense. With nowhere left to go my questions began to change. My negotiations with God turned into surrender—not to the circumstances, but to him! I had no more strength, no power in myself. I simply cried out to God, "Lord, help my son. Show me your purpose for him!" And he did!

Ryan was fighting to live! He hadn't quit! How could his father do any less?

Feelings Don't Define You

Once I decided to fight alongside my son in whatever battles confronted us the question became "how?" How does a man push past the feeling of denial and shock, past feelings of guilt and failure using only his own strength to balance a lifestyle he doesn't choose?

Through the years I began to understand two important truths about myself and this God I've come to know. The first is this:

Just as your child is created in the image of God, so are you![1]

We are often comforted by Psalm 139, which says our children are *fearfully and wonderfully* made and that all of the days of their lives are ordained by God before they were born.[2] The same is true for you, my friend. Here is the second truth.

God uses every circumstance—no matter where you are— for his purposes.[3]

God doesn't waste even our smallest frustration, and he always provides an opportunity for us to shift our focus from ourselves back to him. He is *Jehovah-Rohi*, the God who leads us through times of despair as a strong and patient Good Shepherd leads his sheep.

In Phillip Keller's book *A Shepherd Looks at Psalm 23*, he says that it is no accident that God refers to us as sheep throughout Scripture. "The behavior of sheep and human beings is similar in many ways . . . Our mass mind (or mob instincts), our fears and timidity, our stubbornness and stupidity, our perverse habits are all parallels of profound importance," says Keller. "Yet despite these adverse characteristics, Christ chooses us, buys us, calls us by name, makes us His own, and delights in caring for us." Keller wants us to recognize God's tender care for us—just as we are, with all of our flaws. He assures us that the Good Shepherd is ". . . ever interceding for us; He is ever guiding us by His gracious Spirit; He is ever working on our behalf to ensure that we will benefit from His care."[4]

God Defines You

Have you ever looked into the mirror and wondered . . . *Who is that guy staring back at me?* I have. It takes courage to recognize that the self-sufficient life you spent years building is not your own. It may feel like your life is out of control, when in fact, according to 1 Corinthians 13:12 your life is simply out of focus: "Now all we can see of God is like a cloudy picture in a mirror. Later we will see him face to face. We don't know everything, but then we will, just as God completely understands us."[5]

Brent Olstad

I've come to see waiting rooms differently as I've learned about meaningful waiting and discovered new opportunities. In waiting rooms, I have opportunity to commune with God and find peace in his presence. I can fulfill the needs of others who wait by listening and offering insights in casual conversation. I have opportunity to take stock and contemplate decisions.

Through the years, my waiting rooms have become preludes to joy. While I wait, I see my child grow—this child whose life the doctors said was not viable. He makes me laugh and shake my head in wonder. Now, the waiting room is a reminder of God's care. Each time my son is weighed and measured is a witness of God's provision in his life. His body is not like mine, but his immune system works, his blood still flows and . . . when he is sick, he gets well. Sometimes I wait while his adaptive equipment is adjusted and I give thanks for intelligent technicians who design and manufacture these much-needed aids.

I find comfort in my waiting rooms. Just as God has seen us through other episodes, he will see us through future ones. While I'm not preoccupied with death, waiting rooms open my eyes to the fact that life is precious and it does end. But death is only a prelude to a wonderful new life with God where I picture my son running, jumping, spinning cartwheels, tap dancing and playing the trombone. God has a waiting room. It is found under his wings of love and care. I don't mind waiting there.

Are you beginning to see how circumstances that at first seem to be out of control are actually under control from God's perspective? The journey of following the Great Shepherd does lead to greener pastures.

Jon Ebersole

After years of raising two daughters with cerebral palsy, my façade of perfection finally began to crumble. Those cracks in the "all-about-me" mask I'd been hiding behind exposed the weaknesses that I'd refused to see. But there they were, stealing my joy and the contentment I'd sought as a follower of Jesus. I began to consider the love-hate relationship that Western culture has with weakness. Though we prefer power, we are also drawn to the one we perceive as the underdog in a struggle. We love it when weakness is overcome or people persevere and achieve success.

In reality, this trait comes from the nature of God, who values weakness and humility. First Samuel 16:7 says, "The Lord does not look at the things man looks at. Man looks at the outward appearance, but the Lord looks at the heart." Wow! Talk about an honest assessment of one's self. Jesus also modeled it. There was no pride in him. He never owned a home; instead, he slept outside or at the homes of others. He refused to defend himself from accusations, but laid down what he valued most, his relationship with his Father, in order to become a sacrifice for us. I realized this is what God was asking me to do for my daughters, to lay down my life.

My weakness drove me into myself, but ultimately to the end of myself and into the arms of our heavenly Father. While I did not turn away from God or lose my faith when our twin girls were diagnosed with a disability, I was preventing myself from fully experiencing the love of our Creator. Embracing my weakness has been a process of embracing life's mysteries with gratefulness and trust. I've finally moved to a place of acceptance where I can celebrate human weaknesses. Now I share my journey with other dads with a prayer that it will open their eyes to the peace God wants to give them in their own weakness.

God Always Shows Up

In 2 Corinthians 12:9 the apostle Paul described how God used his own "thorn in the flesh" (weakness) to keep him from becoming conceited. "Three times I pleaded with the Lord to take it away from me," Paul writes, "But he said to me, 'My grace is sufficient for you, for my power is made perfect in weakness.'"

You may be thinking: *If I were a stronger Christian or smarter dad, I could organize, manage or even outsource the disability problems that plague my family.* Paul thought the same. He figured he would surely be a more effective leader without a "thorn in the flesh." But when God showed up, assuring him that his weakness served a purpose, Paul realized that he was not simply a victim of his condition. Neither were Brent or Jon . . . and neither are you! Victims live with a poor-me attitude and a defeated spirit. After talking to God, Paul not only accepted his weakness, he became an "overcomer" in the midst of it. "Therefore I will boast all the more gladly about my weakness," Paul said, "so that Christ's *power* may rest on me. That is why, for Christ's sake, I delight in weakness, in insults, in hardships, in persecution, in difficulties. For when I am weak, then I am strong."[6]

There is no doubt that coping with disabilities can pull a man down about as low as is humanly possible—so low that he has to look up to see bottom. Yet with all that my son Ryan has endured, I'm grateful that together we've learned what it means to be an over-comer. We've witnessed God's presence and power together.

I remember one such occasion that began on a seemingly quiet evening at home. Ryan was only able to be at home eighteen months out of his first three years. That night he sat in front of me on the floor as I cradled him in my arms. I had this brown Naugahyde leather recliner—my favorite chair. The kind of chair your wife's interior decorator insists on donating to Goodwill. Sometimes Ryan would sit with his back against the corner of the room with his face six or seven inches from that chair. He stared at a brown dot on the chair kind of placing himself in a "cocooned state" in order to listen to his head pound. Ryan had endured so much pain in those years that sometimes he would pass out before he would cry, and we would not know the extreme pain he was experiencing until the onset of a seizure.

That day as I held him in my arms, sitting on the floor with my back against the couch, Ryan took a deep breath, rolled his head back toward me and expelled all of his air. He went lifeless in my arms. I quickly rolled him over on his back while my wife ran to call 911.

I got him breathing again and rather than wait for the paramedics to arrive, I strapped him into the car seat and headed to the hospital.

About the time we reached the emergency room driveway I heard Ryan make the same sound. His little arm reached toward me and he immediately collapsed again in his car seat. I ran around to the passenger's side door and pulled him out. His lifeless little two-year-old arms and legs just dangled, no breath came out of his mouth and his eyes just stared at the sky. I remember crying out, "Oh, my God!" I wasn't saying it the way we hear it too often in our society today. I put my head back and begged, *"Oh, my God, don't let this little boy die in my arms. I don't want it to end this way."*

I bolted across the driveway to the emergency room trying to run and force air into Ryan's mouth at the same time, but not doing either one very well. As I burst through the ER doors, it seemed like everything just went silent. It was probably just a few seconds, but it seemed like a very long time. Finally, a nurse who saw me standing there breathing into this toddler's mouth ran over and grabbed Ryan out of my arms. Without a word, she disappeared into the ER's electronic double-doors. I stood there and just shook.

Thankfully Ryan was resuscitated that night and allowed to go home with the admonition that we should expect his attacks to get longer and more severe. And as the doctor told us, eventually the attacks would probably take his life.

Maybe you are currently dealing with uncertainties about your child's health and your family's future. Have you ever thrown your head back and cried out "oh, my God" as I did? Perhaps you have the urge to jump into the car and just drive as far away as possible. Emotional crises are often as traumatic for parents as physical crises are for their children. It helps to stop and picture Jesus standing beside you—the One who took on human form and relates to our weaknesses.

Although I wasn't walking with the Lord as my personal Shepherd during those early years of Ryan's health emergencies, I innately understood that I could cry out to God. And so can you! He knows your voice. In John 10:14-15 Jesus says, *"I am the good shepherd; I know my sheep and my sheep know me—just as the father knows me and I know the Father—and I lay down my life for the sheep."* You can always depend on *Jehovah-Rohi* to hear your cries and lead you through whatever calamity you face.

Prayer's Boot Camp

When life is spinning in circles, we can decide to flee or fight. Go A.W.O.L. as they would say in the military or take a stand! I don't just mean physically fleeing. We can flee emotionally and spiritually as well. A lot of intelligent men have tried to run from God and found themselves on the road to defeat and captivity. This almost happened to one godly father after his beloved sons and daughters were all killed in a natural disaster.[7] He cried out to God in desperation:

> What have I done to deserve this?
> No matter what I do, nothing changes.
> Why won't you answer me?
> I can't take any more of this!
> Where can I get some answers?
> Everything used to be so perfect.
> What good is it to serve God?[8]

Do Job's prayers sound familiar? The Old Testament tells us Job was a righteous man who loved and feared God. Yet when faced with the loss of everything, he tore his clothes and shaved his head in utter anguish. Then he fell to the ground in worship.

What? Hold on a minute. Worship was his response to such tragedy?

In the midst of devastating news, he refused to let his feelings control him. Job cried out to God, and his suffering took a toll on him. Yet he never gave up on God.

Job experienced many of the same trials that fathers of children with disabilities face every day. Dr. Larry Waters, a professor of theology at Dallas Theological Seminary, points out in his book, *Why, O God?* that God allowed Satan to inflict several forms of suffering in his evil attacks on Job. He went through a financial collapse, loss of family, loss of social status within the community, the alienation of family and friends, and, finally, Job lost his health and suffered physical pain, sores, boils, weight loss, trouble breathing, fever, and more.

Can you relate to Job's list? Are you experiencing social, emotional, financial, and physical trials? These trials are part of the process of learning to cope with a child's disability. My friend Frank was forced to sell his family's home and live in a smaller rental in order to qualify for government help for his son's exorbitant medical care and equipment. Daniel, who is a prayer warrior at church, developed debilitating migraine headaches after his granddaughter was born with severe Down syndrome. He hated watching the strain it placed on his own daughter who had to give up her dream of medical school to care for her child.

I've been in Job's shoes myself . . . more than once. I discovered that it is never too late to pick up our weapons of faith and charge the enemy's line. It takes a brave man to run to God in prayer just to get through the day or in some cases . . . the next hour.

Prayer is more than telling God what we want, because he already knows our needs before we ask him.[9] It's admitting we don't know all the facts . . . nor are they necessary for us to continue living a life of faith. In a summary of God's response to Job, Dr. Waters writes:

> God did not address Job's suffering directly during this discourse, nor did he answer Job's attacks on his justice. God spoke to Job about divine sovereignty and omnipotence as demonstrated in the creation of the earth, the sea, the

sun, the underworld, light and darkness, the weather, and the heavenly bodies (Job 38:4-38) . . . God addressed his own justice, but he did not defend or explain it. God did not say he is just and fair in the lives of his creatures. God alone administers and regulates justice—not Job, not the three friends, and certainly not Satan.[10]

Maybe this chapter has been difficult to read because it evokes too many of your own emotions and memories. Well, friend, I'll admit that the only reason I'm sharing my personal struggles with disability is this: *my story is your story*. The disability you are dealing with probably isn't Crouzon syndrome and the circumstances may be different. But you know the stillness of a dark night; you've stared at your sleeping child with a broken heart; you've tried to sweep up your shattered dreams. There have been times when you felt certain that nobody understood. Perhaps, like me, you've tried to be strong for your family and to talk others into believing for the best (when you hardly believed it yourself). I have good news! There is a place to go—your knees—and One to talk with who will answer your questions in his time. There is no circumstance you can encounter that our God has not experienced . . . personally! He watched his Son suffer too. He knows what you are going through and promises to never leave you or desert you.[11]

When life seems out of control, God is always in control. I turn to the Bible daily for answers. Scriptures that I found in my desperation and brokenness, which once annoyed me, are now my most cherished promises. Always take time to listen and take courage from God's Word.

No temptation has overtaken you except what is common to mankind. And God is faithful; he will not let you be tempted beyond what you can bear. But when you are tempted, he will also provide a way out so that you can endure it (1 Corinthians 10:13).

We are on a journey, you and I—along with countless thousands of men like us. Our struggles may be private, but our experiences, emotions, and reactions are often similar. I can affirm that the path is not easy. It can seem unfairly difficult compared to the lives of people around you. However, on that path the façade of life is stripped away, and we see more clearly not how to be a success on the world's terms, but how to be an overcomer in God's eyes.

There is much to this journey that we need to understand. Let's grab hold of the challenge and move forward together.

GROWTH STEPS

1. Your emotions are a gift from God because he made you for himself.

   What has helped you recognize when your feelings are working against you? What would help set you free?

2. In every circumstance of life, God is calling you into a deeper relationship with him.

   When do you find it the most difficult to pray? What would improve your ability and willingness to approach God in prayer?

3. *Jehovah-Rohi*—God My Father leads me through crisis like a strong and patient shepherd.

   Read Psalm 23 and use it as your daily prayer.

CHAPTER **3**

Courage in the Face of Pain and Suffering

BY STEVE BUNDY

*God, who foresaw your tribulation, has specially armed you to
go through it, not without pain, but without stain.*

C.S. LEWIS

My father experienced the Oklahoma oil boom that fueled capi-
talism in the first half of the twentieth century. In films of the
day, such as *Boomtown* and *Oklahoma Crude*, movie stars like Clark
Gable, Spencer Tracy, and George C. Scott portrayed resourceful,
hard-working, self-made oilmen. As a result my father became
quite an entrepreneur. While I was growing up, he started nine
different businesses. His tremendous drive greatly influenced my
young life, since I was usually the first employee in his companies.
I was energetic, readily available, and—most of all—cheap labor.
Before the 1980s oil crisis brought about huge price declines and

turned boomtowns into ghost towns, one of my dad's companies produced holding tanks for oil found in the rich Oklahoma fields. Each oil tank had a square manhole entry on top and a cover that needed to be sealed and bolted down. When I was just a teenager, I ran the machine that drilled holes two inches apart all around the top of the manholes and covers. Each cover needed approximately 50 holes, which was equivalent to drilling through about a half inch of steel. It was one of those tough jobs that made a man out of you! But the key to drilling the holes wasn't found in *my* strength—it was found in the strength of the drill bit.

One day I showed up for work before my father and decided to impress him by jumping right into the day's job. I found a box of drill bits, tightened one into position on the drill and pressed the spinning bit into the steel. Immediately, I heard . . . BAM! BAM! Within seconds, the bit shattered into what seemed like a million pieces! I instinctively jumped under the workbench as metal fragments flew all over the shop. Scratching my head in shock, I figured the drill bit must have been faulty. So I reached my shaking hand into the box again, grabbed another bit, tightened it in the drill and started over. And BANG! The second bit busted and shot like shrapnel in every direction!

When my dad arrived I ran to warn him about the box of defective bits so he could send them back to the store. Dad asked me where I had gotten the bits, and I showed him where I'd pulled the box off the shelf. One quick glance and dad began to explain that I had grabbed the wrong bits.

"These bits look exactly like the bits I always use," I protested.

"While they might look the same," Dad explained, "those bits have not been *tempered*. The drill bits we use on the oil tanks have been tempered by being placed in tremendous heat—hundreds of degrees—until the steel becomes hard enough to sustain the tremendous amount of pressure and tension. Try using a drill bit that has not been tempered and you can forget it! You'll be lucky to make a dent in the steel before the bit explodes into tiny particles."

I'd sure learned that lesson for myself. I also learned that even with a tempered bit the drill operator must be careful not to apply too much pressure at once when pushing through the steel. Too much pressure can dull a bit and eventually destroy it.

The Sonship of Suffering

I've often thought of that day and those lessons in the midst of handling life's pressures. Raising a child with a disability can be stressful on an average day. Then there are days when nothing works right, and we're bent under the weight of the situation. On those days in particular, we need to know that God is the Master Operator of our lives. He knows the right degree of heat required to temper our spirits, preparing us to be able to handle the pressure, especially the pressure that comes with watching our precious children endure pain and suffering. God wants to lovingly temper us through life's high-temperature demands.

Another word for tempering is discipline. The writer of the book of Hebrews tells us to endure hardships as discipline, because "God is treating you as sons. For what son is not disciplined by his father? If you are not disciplined (and everyone undergoes discipline), then you are illegitimate children and not true sons" (12:7-8).

Are you leaning on God as your Father when pressures rise? If so you'll experience the joy and peace of punching through the "steel" of that struggle—without exploding into pieces in the process. This is promised in Hebrews 12:11: "No discipline seems pleasant at the time, but painful. Later on, however, it produces a harvest of righteousness and peace for those who have been trained by it."

The Pain of Peer Pressure

Michael Hoggatt, a special education administrator and social worker, had some lessons to learn when he and his wife, Mandy, adopted their daughter Summer.

Our decision to adopt a child with disabilities from the foster care system was not one we made lightly. As a social worker myself, I understood some of the challenges and potential heartaches. What Mandy and I didn't anticipate was the dismissive nature of some of our family and friends towards Summer's disability, which really hurt! They failed to recognize that she had not only been physically and sexually abused, but she was diagnosed with intellectual and developmental disabilities due to a number of environmental and genetic factors. Instead of loving Summer as she was, they saw her slow speech, maladaptive behaviors and developmental delays as things that needed to be fixed. They had a deep-seated aversion to her disabilities, failing to see that these handicaps were caused by the previous lack of the love and security that Summer needed, which had been denied during her nine different foster home placements before the age of three.

After a few years people seemed surprised that Summer was still disabled. Unfortunately, the negative voices of these so called "well-wishers" began to creep into my own thoughts. I started to doubt my role as her father and blame myself. Maybe we were not giving Summer the right home environment to help her improve. I, too, was tempted to see her as a child who needed fixing.

This idea reared its ugly head at school during Individual Education Plan meetings with developmental services and our regular sessions with her behavioral services team. Maybe we hadn't loved Summer enough. Perhaps a year and a half wasn't enough time. Maybe we weren't the right "forever family" for her or she wasn't the right child for us.

> In the midst of juggling the various services my child needed attitudes of doubt, frustration and anger haunted me. I can't tell you the number of times I said in my own heart, "If Summer would just (fill in the blank with any age-appropriate behavior) things would be so much better."

You can almost feel Michael's pressure rising to the breaking point, can't you? He was slowly buying into the lie that Christians shouldn't have to go through such hurtful struggles. If God was really in control of our families, we could escape pain and suffering, right? Or, to say it another way, "easy is good and hard is bad." But God wanted to help Michael discover that difficult times can also be good. Why? Because it is through pain and suffering that we can truly come to know God.

Paul reminds us that knowing God must be our highest priority. In Philippians 3:10-11 he said, "I want to know Christ and the power of his resurrection and the fellowship of sharing in his sufferings, becoming like him in his death, and so somehow, to attain to the resurrection from the dead." Such a declaration can only be made by a man of courage—one who has been tempered by life's hot spots and shaped under the gentle hand of a Father who watched his own Son suffer. Courage to share in our children's sufferings is not natural—it is a gift from God.

Thankfully Michael did not give in, nor give up, under the pressures of learning how to be Summer's forever father. However he had no way of knowing what deeper waters were still ahead and how much he would need *Jehovah-Rapha*, the God who gives comfort in pain and sickness—who "heals the broken-hearted and binds up their wounds" (Psalm 147:3). Like the thirsty Israelites at the bitter waters of Marah, Michael needed *Jehovah-Rapha* to sweeten his cup and to remind him, *"I am the Lord, who heals you."*[1]

Tempered Steel, Softened Hearts

Michael Hoggatt

A few days after Summer's fifth birthday she began bleeding. After three months of testing, ultrasounds and hospital visits, we received a phone call that rocked our world. The doctor said we needed to get to the hospital where a bed was waiting for Summer on the oncology floor. I'm no medical professional, but I knew enough to know that oncology equaled CANCER. We immediately took Summer to Children's Hospital in Orange County where she underwent another series of tests. The next morning we met a surgeon who confirmed that Summer had Stage IV cancer. One of her kidneys would have to be removed immediately or the cancer, which had already encapsulated the kidney and spread to the lung, could prove fatal. He explained the risks of the surgery and the possibility that Summer could die on the operating table. The surgery was scheduled for the next morning.

Around 2:00 a.m., with Mandy asleep, I left the hospital to pick up some things that we would need for the days ahead. As I drove down the freeway toward our home, David Crowder's song, "How He Loves," was playing on the radio.

He is jealous for me, loves like a hurricane, I am a tree,
Bending beneath the weight of his wind and mercy.
When all of a sudden, I am unaware of these affections eclipsed by glory,
And I realize how beautiful you are and how great your affections are for me.
Oh, how he loves us so—how he loves us so . . .
Oh how he loves![2]

Thinking of God's mercy and affections for me, I could no longer see the road through the tears. I pulled off the freeway to wipe my eyes. In that moment I didn't ask God to fix all of Summer's disabilities or the behaviors that she struggled with. I realized as never before that all I wanted, all I truly desired from God, was that he bring my little girl through this surgery and give me another day with her.

I wanted Summer—not the child she could be, if fixed. Not the one who people thought she ought to be, but rather, the gift of joy that God had given to us just twenty months earlier. I deeply wanted that little girl sleeping in that hospital bed next to her mommy, waiting to undergo something far beyond her comprehension. What I wanted was my daughter, disabilities and all. At that moment, I didn't care if the entire world felt she needed to be fixed. I knew that she was more than enough, exactly as she was. So in the Del Taco parking lot on Freeway 55 in Santa Ana, I prayed that God would remind me daily to be thankful for his gift of Summer.

Following that first surgery, Summer underwent chemotherapy, radiation, CT scans, blood tests, IVs and more surgery. There were many difficult days, but I daily reminded myself that "life is good." Why? Because the joy that our daughter brings to her mother and me (and now to her baby brother) is proof of the sufficiency of God's grace and goodness.

It has been two years since our daughter's initial diagnosis, and I'm happy to say that she is currently cancer-free. Despite our struggles, I continue to advocate for my daughter. I find peace in the here and now by remembering that life—not life measured by the world's standards, but by God's standard—is a gift, as is each day with my daughter.

Encounters with doubts and suffering like Michael's are one of the things that fathers of children with disabilities find in common, although they don't always talk about it. That is not to say that every child with special needs experiences physical pain on a regular basis. Thankfully many of these children are relatively healthy with minimal amounts of physical, medical, or behavioral issues. I have friends with Down syndrome who are always cheerful, and I love spending time with them.

Whatever your journey, I can assure you that God wants to build your character and strengthen your spirit through your role as a parent. God's purpose is to soften your heart toward your family, your friends and everyone you meet along the way.

God uses our children, with or without disabilities, to break down our hard attitudes and to transform us into men of love and compassion. God uses the emotional (and sometimes physical) suffering that we experience to conform us into the image of his Son, Jesus Christ. And as impossible as it sounds, 1 Peter 1:6-7 tells us to be joyful about all this: "In this you greatly rejoice, though now for a little while you have had to suffer grief in all kinds of trials. These have come so that your faith—of greater worth than gold, which perishes even though refined by fire—may be proved genuine and may result in praises, glory and honor when Jesus Christ is revealed."

Ponder the Messiah

You may be thinking, *Okay, I want genuine faith that honors Christ—but I don't want my child to suffer!*

We can all agree that hard times in moderate doses can be a good tonic for the soul. However, the suffering of our precious children is a different story! That kind of stuff can make strong men weak in the knees. Believers and non-believers alike are ready to cry out to God for mercy when their child's life is in danger. And when help doesn't arrive, we want to know why. The key is hidden in the questions we ask when we suffer.

"Why must I endure this uncertainty?"

"Will I ever be happy again?"

"How is this fitting together for the good of my family?" The questions themselves are me-focused.

After more than 45 years as a quadriplegic, author and speaker Joni Eareckson Tada believes that suffering has a way of deflating self. "Suffering is an important part of Christian living that we all should know more about," says Joni. "We want the Lord to just keep the heat down to a manageable level, right? On the other hand, we come unglued if suffering has us at the end of our rope. But this may not be a bad thing. The key is to learn to suffer without dwelling on ourselves. We need to think about a greater suffering and turn to Christ on the cross. Don't ponder 'me' if you're hurting today . . . ponder the Messiah."[3]

Easier said than done! When you've just heard news from your child's doctor, your thoughts don't automatically jump to verses like, *"Don't be anxious about anything, but in everything give thanks"*[4] or songs like "The Doxology." As a friend once told me, it is hard to be *spiritual* when you're turning green and ready to throw up. I can relate to that! How about you?

Adjusting My Focus

One of those "pondering the Messiah" moments in my own test of courage came one night when I was emotionally and physically spent. I was tired of asking God questions about my son's developmental disabilities and getting no answers. At that time, I couldn't yet accept Caleb for who he was—I needed him to be healed. I experienced grief and depression over his condition and felt that my prayers fell silent at heaven's doors. My God seemed impotent as my world crumbled. I labored to interpret Scripture out of my experience, instead of allowing Scripture to interpret my real-life experience.

At that time, my church support group included friends who believed that healing was for all—no exceptions! So sickness, disabilities or ailments all resulted from a lack of faith. This group constantly prayed that my faith would increase, my sins would be confessed and Caleb would be healed. When he was not healed, they concluded that God's favor didn't rest on me or my family. I later discovered that this false teaching focused on the "works of man," and was based solely on one's perfection of faith, rather than on the Word of God. But in my confusion, I was in a dangerous, downward spiral and needed a new, God-centered perspective. One night that perspective broke in on me in a way I could not have predicted.

Many children with special needs have irregular sleeping patterns, and Caleb was no exception. It's as if he was born with no "internal clock" so to speak. It wasn't until Caleb was six years old that we discovered a combination of medicines that assist Caleb in getting a good night's sleep (and us as well). Prior to that Caleb would either go to sleep at irregular hours or wake up crying at irregular hours. Two o'clock in the morning seemed to be his favorite time.

One night when he was two years of age he awoke crying, and I went to his room as usual to comfort him until he went back to sleep. As Caleb dozed off, I lay down on the floor and asked why God had not *fixed* Caleb. I thought: *All the therapies and the doctors' visits, all the special time and attention aren't going to help Caleb's development. They won't fix him! Think of all the glory you would receive, Lord. The testimony of his miraculous healing would reveal your glory to so many!*

I am not one who would claim to have had many "encounters" or burning bush experiences with the Lord. But at that moment, I sensed the presence of God filling Caleb's room so strongly that I cannot fully explain it in words. While I did not hear an audible voice, as clearly as I have ever heard anything, I heard these words flooding my soul: *Son, aren't you glad that I didn't require you to be fixed before I accepted you?* I couldn't move. I couldn't speak. I could only reflect on the words that pierced my heart and mind. In a watershed moment that I can only describe as a revelation, an understanding of the unconditional love of my Heavenly Father burst into my soul.

Son, aren't you glad that I didn't require you to be fixed before I accepted you?

There I was praying for Caleb's brokenness to be fixed, and instead I came to grips with _my own brokenness_. Suddenly it became clear to me that God, the Creator of the Universe, the Incarnate Word made flesh, the Spirit who moves within man, loved _me_ unreservedly regardless of my own performance, abilities or perceived holiness. God accepted me not because of my worth or goodness. It is because of _his_ love and goodness that I can cry out with confidence, "Abba, Father . . . Daddy!"[5]

In the same way, what flooded my soul that night was how utterly selfish, earthly and unloving I had been to my own son, upon whom I had placed such high requirements. With tears running down my cheeks I held my sleeping son in my arms and said, "Caleb, I love you just the way you are, for who you are, and I don't need you to be fixed. You are my son and I'll love you unconditionally from this day forth whether or not you are ever healed." That moment changed my life. Despite my failures, I have been able to accept my son and rely upon God to form me into the father I'd always hoped to be. That night for the first time, I realized that it wasn't Caleb who needed to be healed—it was me.

Reflecting back on that experience in Caleb's room years ago, I am amazed that I could have been so blind to the gift that God gave me in my son. Yes, I can't ignore the real disappointments and challenges that daily accompany life with disability. Our family has experienced a great deal of discomfort and suffering throughout this journey, and as Caleb is becoming a teenager, the challenges continue to increase. As much as I love my son for _who_ he is, I do not always love the *way* he is. But at the same time, he is amazing and continues to be my greatest teacher. Without a spoken word, Caleb touches more hearts for Christ than a lot of Christians I've known.[6]

The Truth About Healing

Several years ago, I had the privilege of teaching on the topic of suffering and disability at a Bible college in Belgrade, Serbia. After sharing my story, a fiery, young student named Philip asked, "Tell me how God can possibly be glorified by *not healing* a person, since such divine healing would surely display his great power." Philip's question is the same one I worked through that night in Caleb's bedroom so long ago. Like many believers, Philip focused his attention on *physical* healing. He couldn't comprehend how God might also be glorified when a person's healing did not take place. But the miracle of healing is that it is first and foremost spiritual in nature. This is not to suggest that physical healings have not occurred, or that a physical healing would not lead people to find Christ.

The New Testament uses many Greek words for both physical and spiritual healing: *sozo, hugies, iaomai* and *therapeuo*. For example, in Matthew 9:22 when Jesus spoke to the woman with the issue of blood, he said, "Daughter, take courage; your faith has made you well (*sozo*).[7] In the next chapter, Jesus commissioned the twelve disciples for ministry and gave them the mandate to "heal (*therapeuo*) the sick" (10:8). These examples are instances of physical healing, where a condition is completely cured. But healing is also for the soul as we find in Ephesians 2:8: "For by grace you have been saved (*sozo*)." Spiritual healing includes a right relationship with God. When a cure was the means to accomplish this restoration, Jesus did so.[8] Otherwise, his ministry was to the heart and soul of mankind.

It is natural to become disillusioned and tempted to abandon all hope when your family is affected by the evil of suffering and disability. Yet evil does exist in our world! And while we may never fully understand the complexity of God's natural order, man is capable of experiencing God's goodness in the direst of circumstances. It is part of the mystery of the Christian faith—a mystery as old as Creation and as fresh as a headline on your iPad.

In the case of Charles Ware's sixteen-year-old son, Matt, God's goodness made the headlines in the Indianapolis Star that read: "Young Athlete Injured, But Not His Faith."

God Gets Glory through Your Sufferings

Dr. A. Charles Ware is president of Crossroads Bible College in Indiana and a board member of the Association of Baptists for World Evangelism and Anchors Away. He and his wife, Sharon, have six children.

I was speaking at a seminary in another state when I got the call about Matt's injuries. "Your son has suffered a C-4 fracture," said the calm, compassionate voice on the phone. "This means he broke his neck." My wife, Sharon, called moments later with news that Matt was being transferred to another hospital, and she would be going with him. After I hung up, a rush of emotion sprang up within me. A flood of thoughts raced through my mind. I felt weak, confused and helpless with my family so far away.

Sitting on the airplane headed home, my tears began to flow. Would Matt live? Would he ever walk, run or play sports again? Who would support my wife through this dark hour? What would I face when I got there and did I have the strength to console my family? Romans 12:1-2 drifted into my mind.

> I beseech you therefore, brethren, by the mercies of God, that you present your bodies a living sacrifice, holy, acceptable to God, which is your reasonable service. And do not be conformed to this world, but be transformed by the renewing of your mind, that you may prove what is that good and acceptable and perfect will of God.
>
> ROMANS 12:1-2 (*NKJV*)

In 1969, shortly after trusting Christ for my salvation, I had presented my life as a living sacrifice to God. Since then God had provided for our family, including bringing Matt to us through an adoption. Reflecting upon those special circumstances that led us to become his parents, my mind felt reassured. God knew Matt before we did and would continue to provide for him now. My responsibility was to continue to be a living sacrifice, even if that meant leaving a ministry that I enjoyed in order to work two or three jobs to meet Matt's medical needs! Peace flooded my being as I rolled all my concerns upon God.

At the hospital Matt lay motionless in the critical care unit arrayed with multiple tubes and wires. After an initial surgery the doctors explained that due to the impact of his head hitting a wall, Matt's fourth vertebrae had shattered and severed his spinal cord. Science had no medical miracle to repair the spinal cord. The prognosis was that Matt would remain paralyzed from the neck down for the rest of his life. Matt had always been an excellent athlete and very energetic. *Paralyzed? Why, when he had his whole life before him?* Over the years, Matt's ADHD had always caused us a great deal of frustration, but now, Sharon and I would gladly trade his bundle of energy for the sedated young man who lay motionless before us.

The Enemy's Disabilities

Satan employs an arsenal of weapons to attempt to discourage, defeat and destroy. Fathers of kids and adult children with cerebral palsy, muscular dystrophy, spina bifida, and brain and spinal cord injuries must keep a vigilant watch to recognize the true enemy. The enemy is not the medical profession, not a bunch of random DNA cells, not the driver who caused the crash, and definitely not *you*! The enemy is Satan!

Some men eventually come to accept this and learn to cope with the thousands of details of raising a child with a disability. Others fail to see this and live defeated lives. It helps to realize that Satan's abilities are also limited. That's right! Our enemy has disabilities! He is not free to do whatever he wishes. If he were, the world would be in far worse shape than it is now. No! God controls evil because he is good.

In chapter 2 we saw this in Job's life. Satan could only do what God allowed him to do to Job and his family. Afterwards, God restored his life. Jesus also declared this to Simon Peter in Luke 22:31-32: "Simon, Simon, Satan has asked to sift you as wheat. But I have prayed for you, Simon, that your faith may not fail. And when you have turned back, strengthen your brothers." Jesus knew Peter would deny him. And in his omnipotence, he knew Peter would boldly preach in his name on the Day of Pentecost and thousands would accept the risen Messiah.[9]

It took some difficult years of living with paralysis for Joni Eareckson Tada to put the topic of evil in its proper place in her life. "Evil can raise its ugly head only when God deliberately backs away for a specific and intentional reason—a reason that is wise and good, even if hidden from this present life," says Joni. "God permits what he hates in order to achieve what he loves—it's just that most of us won't see it until the other side of eternity."[10]

Fortunately God sometimes allows us to witness the climb to victory on the way to eternity, as you'll see in the rest of the story of Charles and his son, Matt.

Your Story Is Not Finished Yet

Charles Ware

Our family saw the hand of God clearly from the first day of Matt's injury. As Sharon wept beside her son's body strapped to the hospital stretcher, Matt looked into his mother's eyes and said, "Mom pull yourself together. Remember, God is in control!"

A sports writer for the Indianapolis Star was on the scene and witnessed this incredible expression of faith. The next day a front-page-article appeared in the Indianapolis Star: "Young Athlete Injured, But Not His Faith."

Matt's statement proved to be a source of constant encouragement to our family and was the beginning of a story that would touch multitudes. Matt slightly moved his left arm the day after we were told that he would be paralyzed from the neck down. Sharon and I were with him twenty-four hours a day. I began to share daily updates with a few friends via email. To our surprise my communications went viral through the social media world. Soon people were praying throughout the U.S., Canada, Italy, Jamaica, Africa, South Africa, India, South America, Holland, and other countries around the world.

Matt's story spread through various other media channels. His injury became the lead story on a local TV news station, front-page articles in the newspapers, and was featured on the Radio Bible Class: Words To Live By on 475 stations worldwide, including Canada, the Caribbean, the Far East (Singapore, Philippines and Korea), Central America (Nicaragua and Guatemala) and Africa (South Africa and Nigeria). He was interviewed for Sports Spectrum Magazine and for a television documentary for young people in Holland and featured at a Billy Graham Crusade held in Indianapolis, Indiana.

During his time in the hospital and rehabilitation he was elevated to what seemed like celebrity status. Letters and cards

67

arrived daily. Friends streamed in. Doctors (in addition to those treating him) frequented his room. Pastors from various churches visited. Even NFL and NBA coaches and players stopped by!

Friends assisted in setting up The Matt Ware Trust Fund to assist with medical needs. Our church collected a single offering of $167,000 and some businesses hosted a banquet, which resulted in donations of $140,000 and a new, handicap-adapted Dodge Caravan! A Christian's construction company assisted in building us a new home and subcontractors bid work below their costs. In July of 1999 we moved into a 3,000-square-foot home on 10 acres of land, debt free!

God is able to heal, but he has chosen to extend his glory through human weakness. Withholding one miracle became an opportunity for performing many miracles! Today Matt is still a quadriplegic, but he navigates his power wheel chair, drives his adapted van, plays video games and has never suffered from depression.

God continues to perform miracles for his glory through a quadriplegic! And as a father, I'm so proud of my son. If the goal is to communicate the gospel and message of faith, I must admit we have done a far better job with a quadriplegic son than we did when he walked. Matt is walking tall by faith, and God is walking with our family.

God can bring good out of any situation—including yours. He sees every moment you put into the care of your child and family. He sees the private tears, the hidden pain, hears the recurring questions. And he sees the love, the compassion, the service you and your family give to one another. Isn't it reassuring that these things "count" with God? Regardless of what you had to give up to care for and accommodate your son or daughter with a disability, your ability to love God and love people has not diminished one iota. If anything, like me, you are probably more aware of those opportunities to love and serve than you ever were before.

When God has you in the refining fire, it's natural to cry out and beg him to turn down the heat. But I and many other men know what's on the other side of that experience: a deeper, richer, more compassionate heart—the heart of our heavenly Father abiding in us.

Something tells me it's worth it.

> Cast your cares on the Lord and he will sustain you;
> he will never let the righteous fall.
> PSALM 55:22

GROWTH STEPS

1. God can use suffering to temper your spirit and strengthen your heart.

   What personal pressure points are currently bearing down on you?

2. Satan can use your family's pain to cause you to focus on yourself.

   What steps can you take to refocus your thoughts and "ponder the Messiah"?

3. *Jehovah-Rapha*—God My Father gives comfort and the final cure for physical, spiritual, and emotional sickness and pain.

   Read 1 Peter 2:24 and use it as your daily prayer.

CHAPTER 4

Courage to
Surrender Control

BY DOUG MAZZA

I have a great need for Christ; I have a great Christ for my need.
CHARLES SPURGEON

In previous chapters we discussed the initial crisis that accompanies the world of disability. We peered through the fog of uncertainty, searching for the courage to face pain and suffering head-on. We grieved the loss of our former lifestyles and considered new steps to regaining the sense of equilibrium we lost when we entered this new world of unfamiliar terms such as: birth defects, autism, cerebral palsy, spinal cord injury, and developmental delay. We heard from Dave, Rick, Brent, Jon, Matthew, and Charles, whose stories are all different with one exception—they were each challenged to surrender to God's plan, even when they didn't understand it. As Jesus himself tells us, surrender is at the heart of the Christian faith.

> Jesus said, "If anyone would come after me,
> he must deny himself and take up his cross and follow me."
> MATTHEW 16:24

Defeat and Surrender Are Not Synonymous

Defeat: 1) to destroy or nullify, 2) to overthrow or conquer, 3) the loss of a contest.

Surrender: 1) to yield to the power, control, or possession of another, to give up or agree to forego in favor of another, 2) to give oneself over to something, as in influence.[1]

The religious leaders of Jesus' day set out to defeat this new self-proclaimed Messiah, but they failed. Jesus vividly modeled the true picture of surrender, especially in his last days on Earth. If you grew up in church, you'll recall seeing paintings of Jesus kneeling in the Garden of Gethsemane. After three years of teaching and traveling with his disciples, confronting the Pharisees' hypocrisy, healing hurting people and feeding hungry crowds, he found himself at the end of his earthly journey. He had, no doubt, witnessed the gruesome, barbaric practice of crucifixion. And being fully human, he prayed with a true sense of desperation, hoping to avoid such an excruciating death. Yet his prayer was also one of submission: "My Father, if it is not possible for this cup to be taken away unless I drink it, may your will be done" (Matthew 26:42).

Skeptics may consider Jesus' garden prayer as the cry of a defeated man. Just twenty-four hours later he was hanging on a rugged cross between two criminals in unimaginable agony of body and soul. But listen carefully and you'll hear his clear announcement of victory—not defeat! John the Beloved, who was there with him, penned his final moments: "When he had received the drink, Jesus said, 'It is finished.' With that, he bowed his head and gave up his spirit" (John 19:30).

The Son of God gave up his life—no man took it from him.[2]

71

If the Son of God had to give over the control of his life to God, his Father, how foolish are we, as mere men, to think that we can control our own lives or deaths?

Don't Try Boxing with God

Dr. James Dobson, founder of Focus on the Family and Family Matters, is a prolific author and master storyteller. One story that has always stuck with me is about the day he was summoned to the pediatrician's office to help his son, Ryan, who was there for a severe ear infection. The infection was so bad that it had adhered itself to his eardrum and could only be treated by pulling the scab loose with a wicked little instrument. The doctor warned Ryan's mother, Shirley, that it would be painful and she would need to hold her three-year-old very still during the procedure. It didn't take her long to decide that this was a job for dad. Dr. Dobson recalls it well:

> I was in the neighborhood and quickly came to the examining room. After hearing what was needed, I swallowed hard and wrapped my 200-pound, 6-foot-2-inch frame around the toddler. It was one of the toughest moments in my career as a parent. What made it so emotional was the horizontal mirror that Ryan was facing . . . making it possible for him to look directly at me as he screamed for mercy. I really believe I was in greater agony in that moment than my terrified little boy. It was too much! What hurt me was the look on his face. Though he was screaming and couldn't speak, he was 'talking' to me with those big blue eyes. He was saying, 'Daddy! Why are you doing this to me? I thought you loved me . . . How could you . . . ? Please, please! Stop hurting me!'[3]

Ryan was too young at the time to understand any explanation his father could have given him. Yet, he was forced to be still under his father's control. The procedure was necessary for Ryan's healing, even if it may have caused him to doubt his father's love for a moment. But his father had not abandoned him. Actually, it was just the opposite! His father had displayed amazing love for his son.

Have you been in Ryan's shoes, feeling betrayed by your Father and desperately struggling to break free from his strong hold in a situation you couldn't understand?

Your arms are too short to box with God. You've heard the old adage, "Father knows best!" In this case, it is true. All the academic degrees on planet Earth won't prepare you to comprehend the unfathomable purposes of God. Man's intellectual apparatus is pitifully ill-equipped to argue with his Creator. Yet, most of us try at one time or another. I finally accepted my own insufficiency during one of my trips to the end of my rope. My son, Ryan, was not responding to treatment, and it appeared that his life was slipping way.

Trading Control for God's Grace

Exhausted, I tried to find a comfortable position in the hospital chair that had been my primary residence for three days. Ryan's heart monitor nearly drove me insane as the green digits indicated a heart rate in excess of 180 beats per minute. My son had yet to reach his third birthday and was fighting for every breath following his tenth brain and skull surgery. A rare chromosomal imperfection had deformed his skull, pushed his eyes nearly out of their sockets, and disrupted his upper respiratory system, even before he was born.

Sitting in that chair I concentrated for a moment on what it felt like to be hugged by Ryan. Despite his deformities his brain had developed to its full size and he had a normal potential intellect for his age. So somehow through all of the pain and suffering, surgeries, and seizures, this little boy had acquired a sweet personality. In spite of his developmental delays, Ryan would race on his hands and

73

knees to greet me when I'd get home and call his name. He always stretched out his somewhat deformed jaw into the warmest, most grateful smile I had ever experienced. But that night in the hospital, it all seemed to be coming to an end. The doctor's words from three days prior kept ringing in my ears. He had sat me down in the children's playroom, locked the door and, with a hint of a tear in his eyes, said, "There comes a time when medical science has done all it can do, and for Ryan I'm afraid that time is now. I don't see how he can live longer than two or three more days."

So there I sat, three days later, with a few family members, living between the resignation of impending loss and the hope of a miracle. I knew that my pleadings with God sat on a thin spiritual résumé. I believed in God. I even believed that Jesus Christ was the Son of God. I just didn't know what that had to do with me. Certainly I didn't have a personal relationship with him—nothing that could be considered intimate. I believed that God surrounded the world and did with each day whatever it was he mystically decided. Like lots of people there were times when I called God into my presence—especially when I was in a tough spot—so I could ask something of him or, maybe stated more correctly, try to negotiate with him. And he seemed like a pretty reasonable God to me, usually willing to do things my way. Just the kind of God many of us want . . . available on demand!

You see I was a guy who had to be in control. But Ryan had completely thrown my life's compass off-kilter. Like every situation I encountered I had put myself in charge of my son's recovery, which was turning out to be the biggest failure of my life. I had exhausted every effort and had no other place to turn with this enormous, painful problem. My pleading prayers were going unanswered, my ability to manage in disarray. What possible purpose could the life of this child have? I had been offered all of the bumper sticker wisdom and pop-Christianity phrases from all manner of people who, frankly, just didn't know what to say. So far, the only role I could see us playing for good was that other people were grateful they weren't us!

Three days after my meeting with the doctor, Ryan was clearly struggling. I couldn't even imagine where his strength to keep up the fight was coming from. I was alone with him at about 4:00 that afternoon. He had been in a coma, completely non-responsive for close to twelve hours when he began to stir. I rose from my chair and leaned forward. He rolled his head toward me, struggled to open his eyes and recognized me as our eyes met. His eyes penetrated me in a way that has never happened before or since—and I will never forget it. He reached for me with what strength he had left, but a soft cloth was wrapped around his wrist and pinned to the sheet, protecting the arterial cutdown which was feeding medicine into his little body. A look came over his face, and I knew exactly what he was thinking: *Daddy, help me! Help me! You're the one who said I would be okay. You're the one I trust; I don't know any power above you.*

And my heart broke. It broke because in that moment I knew I had never actually had such authority, and now I had only moments to make things right. I got down close to my son's ear and for the very first time, I said to him, "Ryan, I can't help you anymore. Jesus Christ is going to take care of you now." With that Ryan slipped back into his deep sleep, and I slipped down onto my knees on the floor clinging to the side of the bed, in a complete emotional collapse.

I now know there were a couple of reasons for that collapse. First, there was the obvious emotion of the moment, which anyone can understand. But there was another reason for that collapse. Have you ever carried something that was unbearably heavy as far as you could possibly go—maybe even farther than you thought you could—and then released it? If you have, then you know the collapse that follows. I had carried the full weight of being in charge of Ryan from the moment he was born. That day in the hospital, for

the first time, I had unwittingly, in faith, released the most important thing in my life to the living Christ. I could feel the weight being lifted off my shoulders. I believe that in that moment of crying
out to the Son of God, Jesus Christ stepped forward and lifted that
sinful cross off my shoulders and took it upon his. Years later after
reliving that moment over and over again, I believe that Christ com-
municated the equivalent of *"I was wondering when you were going to
invite me into this problem, when you were going to turn to me and ask me to
take control."* And by his enormous grace he did, and I could feel it.
Obviously I was still my son's father, but I had finally let God take
his rightful place as the one in charge.

Let Go!

In that moment I learned that God is not going to "elbow" his way
into our lives. He wants to be invited in. The one thing God will
certainly allow you to be in control of is what you are going to do
with his Son, Jesus Christ. Accept him or reject him? Invite him in
or send him away? His grace requires no secret handshake or class-
room time. His grace is immediately available upon your surrender
to him. He'll meet you where you are, do the heavy lifting, and, with
your willingness to receive him as your Lord, provide divine men-
torship in your life to help you develop a deep personal relationship
with him. It just takes one step—and that step is called *faith*! Faith
requires release. God does not want half of your problem or half
of your prayer. Sometimes we hang on to our issues, fears, problems, and needs, as though they were a favorite, old, worn-out pair
of shoes. Jesus wants a relationship with you. If you give him all of
you, he delights in giving you all of himself. He is saying, *"Let go."*

As I sat on the floor of the hospital, nurses came to me and
urged me to go home, since they expected Ryan to make it through
the night. I left the hospital that day a very different man.

Once at home, our family all fell into an exhaustion-induced sleep. At about 10 p.m., the phone rang. As I forced myself awake, I stared at the phone, unwilling to answer it and audibly responding, "No!" to each of five rings, since I knew who was calling. When I finally picked it up, the intensive care nurse said, "I don't know exactly how to explain this, but we moved Ryan's arterial cutdown from his wrist to his ankle. I was doing some paperwork and heard a noise behind me. When I turned around, he was standing up on the bed smiling at me!"

How could that be?! Hours earlier, he was literally on his deathbed. Now, as I arrived at the hospital, I found Ryan lucid and awake, though understandably exhausted from his ordeal. After all the prayers, all the pleading with God, I wish I could tell you that I immediately stopped and thanked God for his miracle. I didn't. I was relieved, glad for our good fortune, and ready to get to the next step of Ryan's recovery. But that moment of releasing Ryan to Christ, combined with the later image of him awake and pain-free, haunted me for a long time without ceasing. I knew something very important had happened. But faith is a journey, and God is patient.

In time, I returned to church to see what God had to say about such things. I sought God's Word as a stranded man seeks water in the desert—not sure he'll find it, but hopeful with every desperate step. And God did not disappoint! On the journey, I found this in Matthew 11:28-30: "Come to me, all you who are weary and burdened, and I will give you rest. Take my yoke upon you and learn from me, for I am gentle and humble in heart, and you will find rest for your souls. For my yoke is easy and my burden is light."

That was strength for another weary step. On the journey, I learned the meaning and value of a personal relationship with the Living Christ, the Christ who defeated death through his resurrection, and the Christ who desires a relationship on a personal level. It was the same Christ who walked across the room and lifted the cross of despair off of my shoulders in Ryan's hospital room that night. My questions were simple: "Lord, I want to know what the truth is about you. If you are who you say you are, tell me plainly. And if you are a God of love, how do I get close to you?" And then one day, there it was—direct, crisp and definitive! BAM! Christ had anticipated my questions, knowing that they are the questions of all humanity. The words exploded off the page, as though they were three-dimensional. Jesus said, "I am the way and the truth and the life. No one comes to the Father except through me. If you really knew me, you would know my Father as well" (John 14:6,7a).

In God's time and with his constant faithfulness and patience the Lord drew me to himself, and I gave him control. He put his arm around me and proved to me that there is only one source of power . . . and it's not me or any person. Was I in charge when I was the senior American executive of a multinational corporation? No. I had responsibility but it was only by God's authority.

Any power that we attain by our own works is doomed to be hollow and empty because it's built on shifting sand. We are all flawed—yet loved by a merciful God. The only real power we'll ever have is offered as a gift and is free for the asking from Jesus Christ, who died on the cross to relieve us of our sins and burdens.

The Winning Formula for a Successful Life

Do you have unanswered questions about your circumstances? Well you need to understand that God will not yell at you from across the street! He wants to be invited into your life so you can experience a personal and intimate relationship with him. The Psalmist describes the security that can be yours, "He is my refuge and my fortress, my God, in whom I trust" (Psalm 91:2). If you have never received Christ as your personal Lord and Savior, ask him into your life today. You were created by him and for him. He has a good plan for your life! Because of our own brokenness, sin and rebellion, we are distanced from God. God is holy and cannot accept sin or evil behavior. Like a judge, he must punish sinful actions. But like a Father, he loves us and forgives us. Because God loves us, he sent his son, Jesus Christ, to pay for our sin by dying on the cross.

Thomas was one of the original twelve disciples of Christ. He traveled with Jesus for three years and watched him in the temple teaching and performing miracles. He knew firsthand that Christ was the Son of God. Yet, after the crucifixion, Thomas doubted. He simply could not accept that after Jesus' torturous death on the cross, he could come back to life three days later. It was too much for him to believe.

After the crucifixion the disciples scattered, fearing for their lives. Later most of the disciples reunited, but Thomas was absent. To their surprise the resurrected Christ came into their midst and says, "Peace be with you! As the Father has sent me, I am sending you." Using today's vernacular you could actually say they had a *strategic business meeting* with a man whom they had just seen crucified and buried!

After Christ left, Thomas showed up. He was too late to witness what had just happened. His reaction is recorded in John 20:24-29.

> Now Thomas, one of the twelve, was not with the disciples when Jesus came. So the other disciples told him, "We have seen the Lord!" But Thomas said to them, "Unless I see the nail marks in his hands and put my finger where the nails were, and put my hand into his side, I will not believe it."

If this kind of skepticism existed in the heart of a disciple who saw the miracles performed, you can begin to understand the doubt many people feel in their circumstances today. But wait, here's the best part of Thomas' story.

> A week later, his disciples were in the house again, and Thomas was with them. Jesus came and stood among them and said, "Peace be with you. Then he said to Thomas, "Put your finger here; see my hands. Reach out your hand and put it into my side. Stop doubting and believe."

I can see Thomas falling to his knees before Christ and the Bible records he said to Jesus the only thing that he could have said: "MY LORD AND MY GOD!" (Emphasis is mine.) Then Jesus told him, 'Because you have seen me, you have believed; blessed are those who have not seen and yet have believed."

That's your opportunity today. To believe in the Christ who wants to walk with you in this life and give you the promise of the eternal life he modeled for you.

The Bible tells us in John 3:16, "For God so loved the world that he gave his one and only Son, that whosoever believes in him would not perish, but have eternal life." Because Jesus himself was holy, he did not deserve to die. As a result, he came back to life three days after dying. When we accept him as our Savior—the one who died in our place—he gives us his Spirit to live in us. The same Spirit that raised him from the dead gives life to our dead spirits.

Accepting Jesus as your Savior is simple. Romans 10:9-10 says, "Confess with your mouth that Jesus is Lord and believe in your heart that God raised him from the dead, and you will be saved." Scripture also says that if we confess our sins, then he will forgive our sins.[4]

Begin by saying this simple prayer:

Father, I thank you for loving me and sending your son, Jesus Christ, to die for me. I do believe that he is Lord and Savior, and that he is alive today. Forgive me of my sins, all the wrong things I have done. Come into my life and change me. I will live for you. I ask for your help to be the man you want me to be. Amen.

Yielding to Adonai—God, Our Master

God is our total authority.

- The songs of David proclaim God's greatness: ". . . You have set your glory above the heavens. From the lips of children and infants you have ordained praise because of your enemies, to silence the foe and the avenger" (Psalm 8:1-2).
- Isaiah spoke of God's power at work: "Every valley shall be raised up, every mountain and hill made low; the rough ground shall become level, the rugged places a plain" (Isaiah 40:4).
- Paul affirmed the keeping power of God: "For I am convinced that neither death nor life, neither angels nor demons, neither the present nor the future, nor any powers, neither height nor depth, nor anything else in all creation, will be able to separate us from the love of God that is in Christ Jesus our Lord." (Romans 8:38-39).

Dying to Self

James Achilles received Christ at age six while attending a Christian day school. Eventually, he chose a vocation in ministry, serving as pastor, music minister and adjunct seminary professor. He and his wife, Deanna, have raised three children. Cathryn, their 21-year-old middle daughter, has a debilitating genetic disorder called ataxia-telangiectasia (A-T), which is a fatal disease. Cathryn's symptoms can mimic muscular dystrophy, cystic fibrosis, cerebral palsy and AIDS. Though A-T causes various neurological effects, it does not alter cognitive abilities, leaving sufferers fully aware of the degeneration their bodies endure. James tells his story here.

> Someone once asked me what it was like raising a child with A-T. I abruptly responded, 'It's like enduring the agonizing death of every dream.' I must have been in a bitter mood that day, because that statement is false. God has fulfilled many of my dreams, but before he could do so, I had to die to a number of life-expectations which were constantly getting trampled underfoot (or pressed under a wheelchair). I realized early in the battle that the death of so many dreams would be a cause for despair unless I let go of my expectations for this life and rooted every hope—immediate and eternal—in Jesus Christ and him alone. Isn't that what God desires for every believer?
>
> As a musician, songwriting has become a daily way to remind myself of the sufficiency of my Savior, and to align my heart with his through prayer. Over time God has answered my request by increasing the challenges of disability and by helping me find "my all in him." His sufficiency has replaced my temporal dreams with the hope of glory and the high call of knowing him. I've claimed Philippians 3:8-9 as my goal: 'For his sake I have suffered the loss of all things and count them as rubbish, in order that I may gain Christ, and be found in him.'

YOU ALONE©
Words and Music by James Achilles

Purify the longings of my soul 'til I desire nothing
more than knowing You.

'Til I delight in clinging to Your side and find
I am satisfied in serving You.

Sanctify the passions of my heart 'til every hope
and dream is found to rest in You;

'Til every thought is with Your Spirit filled, and every passing hour submitted to Your will;

Chorus
You alone, my true First Love, my strength,my joy, my hope—

I find it all in You,

You alone, my Prince of Peace! Come and reign in me.

Teach me now to find my all in You.

James is grateful that his daughter Cathryn knows Jesus and finds courage in his love and grace. She does her best to remain active in church and is an advocate for the A-T Children's Project, a non-profit organization that funds research for a cure.[5] For fun Cathryn works with a mentor/helper to design and make quilts which are usually given away as gifts or sold at fundraisers. Her life has inspired many others, including the ultra-marathoner Tim Borland who ran 63 marathons in 63 consecutive days to raise awareness for A-T.[6]

When I am feeling defeated I like to consider how different Cathryn's life might be without Christ and a believing father, who showed her the way to live her life in service to others. That is an example I want to emulate.

Live for Others—Not for Your Toys

Before the birth of his third child, Will Kantz hadn't had any major hiccups as a parent. He realized that there would be adjustments in moving from one-on-one to zone parenting and a rambunctious boy would need different lines of authority than his sugar-and-spice girls. But he was not prepared for Willson and the way God would use his son to address his own self-centeredness. Cornered by fatherhood, Will felt the nudge of the Holy Spirit and had to examine the intensity of his reactions to Willson's destructive urges.

"Oh no... not again!" This was my youngest son's response when he found his wooden sword with a bite taken out of the tip—another casualty of having an older brother with autism. Though these destructive events occur less often these days, they serve as subtle reminders of my own divine chastening.

Willson's autism forces him to learn in a world of sensory confusion. His ability to perceive through the five senses is severely compromised as vision, hearing, taste, and touch are not always trustworthy—a neurological train wreck that presents the world in an over-stimulated or under-stimulated chaos. One effect of this sensory confusion was destructiveness. I frankly wondered if he would ever get out of the oral toddler stage in which everything is explored by mouth.

To say I was unprepared is a colossal understatement. All I thought I knew about parenting went up in smoke because severe autism rearranges most parenting priorities. We no longer insisted on polite language; we were hoping and begging for any language. We focused less on potty training and prayed that he would stop smearing feces on the bedroom walls. Along with my dreams of a son, it seemed as if my peaceful home and the possessions I'd worked hard to accrue were in a toilet stuck on perpetual flush.

As I sit at my desk my thumb often caresses the deep gouges of Willson's teeth bites in my chair armrests. Our antique heirlooms and furniture pieces have been gnawed, bitten, tasted, yanked, bent, thrown and otherwise tested. My exercise machine

84

is the only item unmarred because it's made of steel. Only now as Willson nears age fifteen are we testing his waning destructiveness with the purchase of some nicer things. But during those destructive years, God showed me that the love of self and toys were strongholds that I needed to confront as the sin of idolatry. My toys and treasures were a hindrance to my walk with Christ, who calls us to devalue material things and see people as invaluable.

My son is a gift . . . just like he is . . . especially like he is. As I have shifted my materialistic outlook to a simple appreciation for my son, I've slowly adopted Christ's priorities. His priorities can lead to Christian maturity and a solid peace—one that the world (and all the stuff it offers) cannot take away. I thank my son for this gift.

Keep Walking

When we refuse to turn our burdens over to God completely, we don't put him in charge—we dishonor him. We're telling Christ that he died in vain. Instead, we must set aside our earthly pride and say, "Lord I turn this problem, this disability, my burdens over to you." Only then do we glorify God and allow him to show us the way through. We will become empowered by the Holy Spirit, the same awesome power who created the universe. You too can be empowered by a living, loving God that was willing to send his Son to Earth to endure as much pain and suffering as this world has to offer. Christ demonstrated, in the most graphic way, that he understands our pain—and he also demonstrated the ultimate victory! He promises to show us the way out of all our troubles if we turn them over to him, yield control, and seek his will in all situations.

In 1 Corinthians 10:13 we read: "God is faithful; he will not let you be tempted beyond what you can bear. But when you are tempted, he will also provide a way out so that you can stand up under it." When you trust him completely to bring you through, that light you see at the end of the tunnel is not a train coming at you; it's a promise from the Bible that "...in all things God works for the good of those who love him, who have been called according to his purpose" (Romans 8:28). I've discovered that all of God's promises are available to all of God's people all of the time. And in the end, he promises to exchange our deserved death for victory and life forever in him. Now that's a deal!

Never, Never, Never Quit

Congratulations on making it through four chapters of a book you probably didn't expect to be on your reading list. This wasn't one I ever expected to write either. But here we are together, four chapters deep. Let's not quit now! It is reported that Winston Churchill once said, "Never, never, never, never, give up!" Quitting is not surrendering. The time may come when you just want to quit and leave disability behind to start fresh on a different plan for your life. *Don't!*

Join God's Health Club plan. Accept Jesus, read your Bible, have quiet times with the Lord, and you'll be renewed physically, mentally and spiritually. Commit to believing God's promises which requires faith . . . and faith requires surrender . . . and surrender provides strength . . . and strength will produce endurance.

God has shown us throughout history that he never intended for us to be in charge; that's God's role. Failure and frustration come from our unwillingness to accept the role we were created to fill. Surrendering to God by following Christ and trusting his leadership is the first step to realizing his purpose for your life.

God loves joy—he invented it! But for the Christian, our destination in life is more than joy—it's contentment. Paul learned this truth by surrendering his all to Christ. He said in Philippians 3:12-13, *"I have learned the secret of being content in any and every situation, whether well fed or hungry, whether living in plenty or in want. I can do all things through Christ who gives me strength."*

Giving up control of my life was one of the hardest things I've ever had to do. But I had to do it or I wouldn't have made it through. God knew the lessons I needed to learn. He knew how much I would resist, and he knew what it would take for me to yield responsibility to him for my son, my life, my future—everything. Perhaps you are still pondering these stories of surrender. Whether you have made such a commitment in the past or not, I encourage you to embrace it now. Only when we let go will we receive all that God has for us—including the love and strength to thrive in the midst of the greatest challenges. It is the best exchange you'll ever make.

GROWTH STEPS

1. Men are not naturally conditioned to surrender.

   Think of a time when you felt trapped by an impossible situation. Now, consider the possibility that God was holding on to you, keeping you from defeat and asking you to surrender to him.

2. Sin is common to all men, an inherited condition due to Adam's rebellion in the Garden of Eden. Jesus Christ, the only Son of God, is the only cure for sin.

   Is Jesus on the throne of your life? Do people describe you as a Christ-follower by the way you live your life?

3. God is faithful. You can trust him with the innermost parts of your heart.

   Praise God for the plans he has for you that you can't yet see. Surrender your desires and hopes to him, being confident in his purposes for you.

CHAPTER 5

Courage to Grasp the Servant's Towel

BY STEVE BUNDY

*Life is an exciting business, and it is most exciting
when it is lived for others.*
HELEN KELLER

Whether Brian Williams or Diane Sawyer, today's news anchors often interview people they call "everyday heroes." Some heroes bravely perform acts of courage that save people in harm's way, such as the first responders in the Boston Marathon bombings. Others stand up under extreme pressure to speak out against injustices, such as Nelson Mandela, who spent twenty-seven years in prison to protest apartheid in South Africa. Sometimes fathers of children with disabilities are called heroes, although most of them would reject the title, preferring to be seen simply as dads who love their children.

One such man is Chris Cady, winner of the 2011 Military Fatherhood Award from the National Fatherhood Initiative. Chris is a single parent and a Navy officer, serving his country by delivering sensitive documents all over the world. At the same time, Chris is the primary caregiver for his teenage son Josh. Road-warrior occupations can be hard on families, and Chris's job is especially difficult on Josh, who has severe disabilities. A devastating virus, present at Josh's birth, left him deaf and blind. He also has epilepsy and receives his nourishment through a feeding tube. Yet Chris embraces Josh's many challenges, serving as a hands-on dad as much as possible. When he does travel, a group of family and friends form a care team to take responsibility for Josh. Such support frees Chris to not only do his job, but also to serve as a member of the White House Champions of Change round table on fatherhood.[1]

Maybe you're thinking, *I'm not in any danger of being called a hero. Most of the time I feel more like a zero.* Sure, your neighbor Joe thinks you're a selfless guy, and your golf buddy Chuck calls you Superman, but they don't have a clue about the never-ending lowly tasks that are required to get your child through a regular day. If your son has physical impairments, you may help him with dressing, exercising, feeding, brushing teeth, and toileting care. If your daughter has a developmental disorder, her therapy schedules may feel like a full-time job. Many dads fight fatigue like soldiers on a secret mission, and as if that isn't enough, they're also expected to know about medical trends, diets, and treatments.

Depending on a man's personality, these demands can either bring out the best in him or magnify his character flaws. Some fathers turn all the work over to their wives and as a result end up carrying a guilt trip the size of a Boeing 747. Other men grab the reins of their child's care like a racehorse jockey bolting out of the gate—and soon discover that they're too tired to go another lap. Some families can afford to hire nannies and caregivers to serve their children's needs. Others, like Chris, are blessed to have a support system. Sadly, these examples are more often the exception than the rule.

"I hate to admit it," says Adam, father of triplets with special needs, "but there are days when I feel more like the hired help than a dad. Then, when I hear a sermon on serving my church and community, I cringe, thinking surely God knows that I have my hands full at home."

I've had days when I've felt like Adam; haven't you? Servanthood doesn't come naturally to most men, especially when we've been taught all our lives to be the breadwinners. We've gone to college, worked our way up in a company, or started our own businesses. We've earned places of respect in the workplace. Even when we have volunteered in the community, it's not as tough as taking care of an adult child with a disability who can't feed or bathe himself.

Secrets of Service

Though serving may not come easy, I've discovered some secrets about God's call to service that I want to share with you in this chapter. Before I do, let's confront some faulty thinking that can hold us back.

Some men struggle to accept the call to serve because they have never learned to accept help from others. They reason, *since I wouldn't like to do that [fill in the blank] for somebody, I don't want anyone doing it for me.* This thinking is flawed because, like many truths in Scripture, God's view is the opposite of the world's view. For example,

To gain your life, you must lose it.
To receive, you must give.
To live is Christ and to die is gain.
To be strong, you must be weak.
To experience eternal life, you must have the faith of a child.
And to be great, you must first be a servant.[2]

Did you catch that last point? To be great, one must first be a servant. I can't think of a more countercultural statement than one that reverses how we perceive greatness in our culture—going from being the one who is served to the one who serves others. But Jesus wasn't about affirming culture. He was focused on displaying the character of God— One who appeared in the flesh as a servant.[3]

You may recall Jesus' final act at the Last Supper prior to his arrest and crucifixion. As the disciples gathered in the Upper Room around the table, they each jostled for the most honorable seat. It was customary that a servant be in the house to wash their feet upon entering as a symbol of cleanliness and honor. But no servant was present, and no disciple dared to serve in this manner. Imagine the disciples' surprise when Jesus, without saying a word, humbly arose from his seat and placed a servant's towel around his waist. Then, one by one, he began to wash his disciples' feet. Why? In his own words: "If I then, your Lord and Teacher, have washed your feet, you also ought to wash one another's feet. For I have given you an example" (John 13:14–15, *ESV*).

I don't know about you, but serving just does not come naturally to me. Like the disciples, my natural bent is to push past the wash basin and towel and to find my place at the table. "Honey, is dinner ready?" "Where are my clean socks?" "Did you get to the cleaners?" "I am out of shirts." "Have you bathed Caleb?" "Can you help Jaron get to sleep?" You get the picture. Serving our families is not about what feels good or comfortable at the moment, it's about an unwavering commitment to walk in the steps of our servant Savior. It's about picking up the towel and washing smelly feet because our love and passion for Jesus is greater than any earthly seat of honor.

I had an experience in college that left a lasting impression on me. I attended a Christian college at which the Bible and missions courses were central. Like most college cafeterias, the dining hall had a cleaning station where students and staff dropped off dinnerware and trays. Many students who wanted to offset tuition costs were in the student work program. Unfortunately, assignments were given based on job availability rather than according to preference. After lunch one day at the tray return, one student worker was loudly expressing his extreme dissatisfaction with his role as a dishwasher. He was not only vocalizing his dissatisfaction with the messy job but was also angrily tossing trays and plates while making sharp comments to students about how they were placing their trays as they passed by.

What happened next took me completely by surprise. I noticed that standing right behind me in line was Professor Harold Brokke. Dr. Brokke, a legend on campus, was one of the first to teach at the college after it was founded. Moreover, he had become the college's president before retiring from that role and later returning in a faculty position. Noticing the disgruntled worker, Dr. Brokke paused for a moment, clearly taking in the rant, as did the rest of us. Then he made his way back to the cleaning station. I thought, *Oh, this is going to be good. I don't want to miss this. He is going to light this student up!* But what happened next did not involve a rebuke or a sharp verbal correction. In fact, no words were used at all. Instead, Dr. Brokke took off his suit jacket, rolled up his sleeves, and simply began to clean dishes alongside this young man. All eyes fell on Dr. Brokke and the student. There was no need for words because the lesson was evident to all of us.

. . . .

How has God called you to serve your family? What service opportunities have you missed out on because you're convinced that it's not your job to do the dishes or the laundry or the shopping—or whatever needs to be done? God has called us all to get out of our comfort zone and put the servant's towel around our waists.

Measuring Your Comfort Zone

As Christians, we have the example of Jesus Christ, who stepped out of the comfort zone of the religious leaders of his day. He lived in ways that clearly revealed God's definition of a servant. He often surprised his disciples by stopping to touch people who were poor, sick, and disabled. By making those whom society passed by a priority in his ministry, he demonstrated God's grace and compassion for "the least of these."[4] Yet even some of Jesus' closest friends had trouble grasping this teaching.

In Matthew 20:20–28 the mother of Zebedee's sons pressed Jesus to favor James and John by allowing them to sit by his side in his kingdom. Jesus asked these two if they could drink the cup of suffering that he would drink, the one his Father had prepared for him. He reminded them that it was the rulers and high officials of this world who set themselves over other men and flaunted their authority. Then he warned, "Not so with you. Instead, whoever wants to become great among you must be your servant . . . just as the Son of Man did not come to be served, but to serve" (20:26, 28).

In the previous chapter we discussed what it means to give ourselves to God by accepting Jesus Christ as the One who gave his life for us. As Christians, we grow by stepping into Christ's footprints in the sand and *giving* our lives in service to others. In acts of sacrificial service, we begin to understand what Jesus asked his disciples that day: "Can you drink the cup I am going to drink?" (20:22).

Henri Nouwen is one of the most popular spiritual writers of our time. He taught at Yale and Harvard before spending the later years of his life as a member of L'Arche Daybreak in Canada, where he served people with disabilities. In his book *Can You Drink the Cup?* Nouwen describes the importance of the cup as a life symbol. For example, you may have a family shelf of trophy cups earned in sports, recitals, or through other achievements. These cups represent success or fame. Or maybe you invite friends over for drinks and use your ordinary, everyday cups. These cups signify friendship and hospitality. In history some cups have represented doom, such as Socrates' poisonous cup or the cup Joseph's servants found in Benjamin's sack when he and his brothers were leaving Egypt.[5] If that cup had been stolen, it could have cost the thief his life. Nouwen suggests that Jesus had a different kind of cup in mind:

> The cup that Jesus speaks about is neither a symbol of victory nor a symbol of death. It is a symbol of life, filled with sorrows and joys that we can hold, lift, and drink as a blessing and a way to salvation. . . . At one moment it might seem so easy to drink the cup, and we give a quick yes to Jesus' question. Shortly afterwards everything might look and feel quite different, and our whole being might cry out, 'No, never!' . . .
>
> Drinking the cup is an act of selfless love, an act of immense trust, an act of surrender to a God who will give what we need when we need it . . . Jesus' inviting us to drink the cup without offering the reward we expect is the great challenge of the spiritual life. It breaks through all human calculations and expectations. . . . Drinking the cup that Jesus drank is living a life in and with the spirit of Jesus, which is the spirit of unconditional love.[6]

Secret #1: Love Inspires Service

God is love.
1 JOHN 4:16

God has a significant servant's role for each man to fulfill in his family, church, circle of friends, career, and community. And his role is often revealed through his children.

At the age of nineteen, Kim Miller was diagnosed with a random deletion to her first chromosome. Her fine motor skills, such as writing and speaking, are impaired, but she is able to communicate with a portable speech computer. Kim struggles with change, loves books, hates waiting in line, and expresses her displeasure with loud, annoying whines. Some have described these wailings as "nails on a chalkboard." Yet her father, Paul Miller, executive director of seeJesus Ministries,[7] credits his daughter with teaching him about love and service.

One of Paul's biggest lessons came when he decided to give his wife a well-deserved break by taking Kim with him on a weekend trip. The two of them would travel on Friday, Paul would speak on Saturday, and they'd return home Sunday. This father-daughter adventure sounded simple enough—until the problems began:

> While Kim and I waited for the shuttle bus in long-term parking, Kim discovered that her mom had forgotten to pack her a book for the plane ride. As I stood there holding two suitcases and a box with "seeJesus" on it in large, red letters, Kim began to whine while other travelers watched. I could have throttled her. I considered turning the box around to hide the lettering.
>
> Kim finally stopped whining, but only because I was yelling at the bus driver who was closing the rear door on me as I helped Kim navigate the step. In the terminal, the check-in baggage lines stretched forever, so I lugged our suitcases and the box upstairs to security. As soon as we got in that line, they closed one line and combined the others. Kim began to whine again. My seeJesus box wouldn't fit through the scanner and it required a separate scan by a scrupulous guard.
>
> With twenty minutes to go, I discovered that our gate was one terminal over. I contemplated running with Kim while carrying our luggage, but then I saw an electric cart. Kim laughed as we went whizzing off.
>
> Just as we got settled into our seats and Kim began listening to a CD, the pilot's voice came over the intercom saying please turn off all electric devices. She not only had to turn off her CD, but also her speech computer. Her whine started at a low pitch and quickly turned into a temper tantrum when the pilot said we were twelfth in line for takeoff. All Kim's hot buttons had been pushed: no book, schedule changes, and waiting!

While some may ask, "What's the point? Why would Paul take Kim on such a trip? Wouldn't her needs be best served if she were left comfortably at home?" Paul says no!

> It all boils down to who God is and what his heart is like. In Scripture, God is known by what he does. First John 3:16 says, "This is how we know what love is: Jesus Christ laid down his life for us." Without Jesus' sacrifice, we would not know this love. For me, taking Kim on that trip was a way of laying down my life for my wife Jill, who enjoyed a stress free and restful weekend.
>
> When you speak publicly, you are still at the center, even if you are talking about serving Jesus. However, just the day before at the bus stop, the security line, and on the plane, I had been powerless to stop Kim's whining—and believe me, those crowds certainly weren't respecting and looking up to me. I felt inadequate, and I was inadequate. In his grace, God gave me an opportunity to look foolish. He reminded me what I am without him.[8]

A man who willingly enters into the fellowship and service of Christ comes to know God and himself better as well as love others without limits.

Secret #2: Servanthood Leaves a Legacy

God is not unjust; he will not forget your work and
the love you have shown him as you have helped his people
and continue to help them.
HEBREWS 6:10

As the pastor of a congregation in Phoenix, Arizona, Mark Mucklow keeps a full schedule. Like most leaders, Mark tries to be available when people need him while constantly keeping his own family a priority:

> Although I had preached that disability could strike anyone in countless ways at any time, I just assumed that because my other children were born healthy, they would never experience major health issues. I was wrong. The same summer that we were re-joicing over Joel's health, my wife began noticing that something was wrong with Elizabeth. I went down the road of denial and honestly thought my wife was over-reacting.
>
> Liz is our third child and second daughter. At age seven, she was certainly the least coordinated of our children, but we fig-ured there were some people who were just not as coordinated as others. We even teased Liz about being a little clumsy, but in time, we noticed that she had far less balance and coordination than her peers. Eventually, we decided to talk with our family's doc-tor about our observations. On his recommendation, we found a neurologist who agreed to evaluate Liz. After he spoke with her and asked her to walk towards him, he confirmed our fears that something was not quite right. He soon determined that our daughter had a rare condition called Friedreich's ataxia, or FA.
>
> FA is a debilitating, life-shortening, progressive, degenerative neuromuscular disorder. One in every 50,000 people in the U.S. develops Friedreich's ataxia. There is currently no cure or effec-tive treatment for FA. Symptoms are the loss of coordination, fa-tigue, vision and hearing impairment, slurred speech, and serious heart conditions. FA slowly worsens, causing patients problems with performing everyday activities. Most need to use a wheel-chair by their teens or early twenties.
>
> As a father, I believe it is my God-given responsibility, among other things, to be my family's provider and protector. Liz's diag-nosis struck me as something that could eventually keep me from

97

being able to perform those responsibilities for my daughter. I felt forced to depend on God more than ever.

The amazing thing was that eight years before Liz was diagnosed I'd had the privilege of helping my church start a disability ministry. When our hearts were breaking with this news, my wife and I had a rich reserve stored up from working among our church's families with disabilities. God knew we would one day need the wonderful training Joni and Friends had provided us. We knew lots of impressive families and had heard their inspiring testimonies. I had attended Joni and Friends Family Retreats and Through the Roof Conferences. I can't overstate the benefits of having God prepare my heart, in ways I was not aware of, to be Liz's father.

Caring servants—volunteers, teachers, and caregivers—with willing hearts and hands had left a legacy for Mark's family to follow. He was able not only to care for his daughter in the midst of the challenges but also to triumph through his own weakness to experience God's strength. While he had always believed biblically that God would bring glory to himself through Liz's disability, those in his church family were the ones who showed him God in the flesh. Mark says,

> We've seen the Lord glorified through Liz's life. She knows that God has granted this especially to her for his purposes. We have watched our daughter mature through her disability and praised God when he has used it for kingdom purposes. Today Elizabeth is a vibrant witness for Jesus wherever she goes. God continues to greatly bless her faithfulness. Our entire family is enriched by God's gift, and we will never be the same.

Mark could have gotten trapped in the "poor me" syndrome, given up, and left his position as a pastor. But he had already been humbly serving others and was able to leave a legacy for Liz and his family.

One of the names for God is *Jehovah Nissi*, the Lord My Banner. It means "God wins over our flesh and brings lasting victory." Isaiah prophesied that the "Root of Jesse" (Jesus) will stand as a banner for the people—a legacy.[9]

Secret #3: Service Is Part of Healing

I (Jesus) no longer call you servants,
because a servant does not know his master's business.
Instead, I have called you friends.
JOHN 15:15A

It may sound strange to say that serving helps bring about one's own healing, yet this profound mystery is seen in Scripture. In Luke's Gospel the apostle tells the story of a "sinful woman" who washed the feet of Jesus with an expensive perfume and her own tears.[10] Although she was ridiculed by some who saw her action as lowly and wasteful, Jesus praised her by declaring that she was forgiven of her sins and on a path of healing. Her act of service displayed her own brokenness as well as her willingness to let go of pride, arrogance, and self-reliance. This example should challenge our ego and humble us to receive healing from the One who gives to all freely.

Over the years I've been privileged to serve alongside Joni Eareckson Tada. People travel from all over the world to get just a moment with this inspiring lady. Many who are attracted to Joni have themselves suffered and feel that Joni identities with their journey. They often share their issues and pain with her, knowing that she will remember to pray for them. Joni is so gracious to every visitor. I've watched her listen to people's stories, offer words of encouragement, and take a moment to pray with them. Then she invites them to serve others. If there is a mutual acquaintance or a need that Joni is aware of in a person's hometown, she asks that individual to pray about meeting that need. At times, she might ask someone to visit a hurting friend in a certain hospital or care facility. And she often requests daily prayer for her own need or for our ministry at Joni and Friends.

After watching Joni's pattern of redirecting people to acts of service, it finally dawned on me what she was trying to achieve. It came as I listened to her testimony one day to a group of students. Joni said that by taking her eyes off herself and serving others, she had found the healing power of God in her own life. When we focus on our needs and problems, we prolong the healing process and give in to a "poor me" attitude of self-centeredness. God's healing touch, on the other hand, moves us into something greater than ourselves—acts of service to others. Joni has redirected people to acts of service for their own good.

. . . .

One of the final classes I took to complete my graduate degree in organizational leadership concluded with a "Leadership Challenge Weekend." I have since renamed it the "Weekend from Hell." It was the end of March, and the weekend consisted of spending three days and nights on Mount San Jacinto in Southern California. Mount San Jacinto is about 10,000 feet in height. It was recommended that we bring proper clothing for cold weather, including ski gloves, jacket, and head gear.

Now I am a native of Oklahoma, and for those who may be geologically challenged, Oklahoma does not have any mountains. There are some nice hills that we like to call mountains, but they're not! Needless to say, in my experience March has been quite warm, so I decided that a good old pair of gardening gloves and a light jacket would do just fine. There was no way I was about to dish out hundreds of dollars for clothes I would probably never wear again.

The first sign of trouble came when we stepped out of the gondola that had taken us 8,500 feet up the mountain. The sound of *crunch* under my foot, the freezing wind hitting my face, and the blinding white powder everywhere made me quickly realize that I had miscalculated the odds of a warm weekend on the mountain. It was kind of like General Custer's assumptions leading up to the Battle of the Little Bighorn. "Ah, how many Indians can there be?" Answer: "A lot more than you assumed." I was in trouble but determined to see the weekend through.

We hiked another 800 feet and set up camp at around 9,300 feet elevation. I was thrilled at the prospect of climbing into a warm tent and snuggling into my sleeping bag to defrost my toes. After finding a suitable tent site, our leader handed me a tarp and a pole. *Surely these are ground cover for the tent to provide more warmth,* I thought. But as I waited for the actual tent, he just pointed to the tarp and pole in my hand and said, "That is your tent!" That night on the mountain, I felt like a shrimp appetizer lying on a bed of ice! All that was missing was the cocktail sauce.

Three days later I was beyond ready to make my departure from the mountain. However, we had to conquer one more challenge before our descent, which entailed taking turns leading the entire team to the mountain's summit. At that point my ego kicked in, and I was ready to kick butt! *Let me lead,* I thought. *I'll get us up and back quickly and safely and still demonstrate quality leadership principles along the way.* Unfortunately, my lot fell to bringing up the rear. But the leader assured me that I'd get my opportunity to lead.

After some time of climbing, I'd had my fill of bringing up the rear. By this time some of the women had given up and were turning back. One lady, who had sprained her ankle, felt she couldn't go any farther. Her moans eventually turned into tears. I soon found myself being the comforter, encourager, and sounding board for those lagging behind. Just short of the summit, the leader felt we needed a break. By this point I was in a self-induced pity party. We were near the top, and I had not been given a chance to lead. Instead, I was stuck at the back taking care of whiners.

I began to internally mull over my complaint until it became an outright rant to the Lord, covering the unfairness and suffering that I'd had to endure over the years. It went something like this: "You know, Lord, this trip is a good summary of my life. It just sucks! I am always behind the scenes, last to the front, taking care of the messes and cares of life that few others have to deal with—it is so unfair." Now I didn't articulate how I was defining "cares," but I was thinking of the challenges with my son Caleb. Few people know the trials of autistic behaviors, non-verbal communication, daily diapering and toileting, feeding, changing, and so on—all wrapped up in one child. I was seeing my son's needs as a duty instead of as an opportunity. In other words, my attitude was "I must" rather than "I get to" serve. As a result, I realized that I was still working through resentment issues.

· · · ·

Fortunately, that isn't the end of my Leadership Challenge Weekend story. As I sat on a rock complaining to the Lord, an internal voice spoke to me. Instantly, I knew it was the Lord's. In a loving rebuke he seemed to say, "Yes, Steve, you are struggling. You are in the back, and you're serving with no spotlight or recognition. You think you should lead, but that is a position I grant to those who have first learned to serve from behind. I gave you Caleb, and it's your honor to serve him. I've entrusted him into your care. You will learn to lead others by first serving your family, not in spite of your family."

This was a powerful revelation for me. On top of that mountain, I realized that my strengths and healing would actually come through service.

I've also learned that we can actually hide in the spotlight. You heard me right—men hide in the spotlight of business, activities, accomplishments, being out front, and carving a path. These can keep us from honestly dealing with real emotions and issues of pain, anger, and unhealthy lifestyles. But when we can slow down, stay in the shadows, and serve behind the scenes, we can watch God's work of healing our hearts and souls. It's where God wants us—before we can lead, we must be in a place of service, where he can mend the pain that lies beneath the surface.

Secret #4: Service Brings Glory to God

If anyone serves, he should do it with the strength God provides,
so that in all things God may be praised through Jesus Christ.
1 PETER 4:11

Most of us have seen the artistic rendering of Jesus at the Last Supper with the bowl of water and the servant's towel over his arm.[11] The picture is a drama of conflict. Jesus had already predicted his own death and the hard life that his disciples would face in the days to come. Yet the disciples were still unclear about their purpose and how they would accomplish all that they had seen and heard in the three years that they had walked with the Lord. But as they felt the hands of Jesus washing their feet and patting them dry, there was no doubt about their gratitude for their leader who loved them enough to perform this lowly service. Surely the glory of God must have filled that room in those hallowed moments.

Richard L. Gathro serves as the director of Pepperdine University's Washington, D.C. program and the Institute for Public Service and Policy Development. His adopted son, Will, was born in 1985. Rich and his wife Kathy had planned to name him Ian, after Rich's

Scottish heritage. But when Kathy looked at the child, she said, "Let's call him Will, as he will need a strong will to make it in life." She was right.

Within a few months of his birth, the medical community confirmed that Will had cerebral palsy and probably would never walk or function well. Thankfully, God had something else in mind. He provided the caring support of the special-education community. Will's preschool teacher even became like part of their family, and Rich and Kathy had dear friends who continue to love Will to this day. The greatest experience for them was watching Will's incredible determination. Undaunted by bruises and stitches, he eventually walked at age five. He banged himself up so many times that he was on a first-name basis with the local emergency room staff. He never gave up, and he never complained.

Will is now age twenty-seven, and Rich still carries around his son's softball card that reads "Age 10, Height 4' 2," Weight 73 lbs., Position Shortstop, Team Cardinals." When Will was young, a group of parents who all had children with special needs formed a Little League division called Challengers. Rich gladly served as one of the coaches and always felt that the happy faces of the boys and girls made it all worth it. Along the way, he also realized that he was being changed into the likeness of Christ:

> After incredible grief in Will's infancy and many sleepless nights, we just needed to open our eyes to the blessing that was intended for us. The road has been incredibly difficult, challenging us in every way, challenging our marriage, challenging our identity. I wish that I could say that it was easy and rosy. It's been incredibly painful. But, it has been a worthwhile journey.
>
> I work in Washington, D.C. which is somewhat of a study in contrasts, where our largest homeless shelter in the city is located two blocks from the Capitol . . . power and powerlessness right

in our faces. Numerous encounters with the homeless take place each day as I depart the subway. One day I noticed that a major change was taking place in me. Instead of ignoring these people I noticed that I knew them by name and was developing friendships. You see, I owe this to Will. He taught me that every human being matters, and not to just look at the outside of a person. Each person bears the image of God.

When Will was a teenager, he joined a Young Life program for youth with disabilities called Capernaum Partnership, founded by Pam Harmon. The club was the first of its kind on the East Coast. Rich and Kathy, who had been at their wits' end when their son joined the club, credit the program with saving Will from his deep despair, loneliness, and anger toward God. When Will was invited to speak to the board of Young Life in Colorado, he used his assisted speech device to say that he was no longer lonely because he had many friends who loved Jesus. He now resides in a terrific group home in Texas called Cornerstone Ranch, founded by people with Young Life roots. Recently he accepted a leadership role in Capernaum Partnership.

Will's life sheds God's glory on everyone who knows him—especially his parents. Rich now says, "My definition of courage is being scared but tackling the challenge anyway." Good advice for dads everywhere!

. . . .

Serving others, beginning with our family, brings the added benefit of healing to our souls. God has designed us to give to others—and when we serve in his name, we are open to receiving his healing touch in return.

GROWTH STEPS

1. God has given you spiritual gifts to use in his service.

   How are you discovering and using your gifts?

2. Servants don't seek glory for themselves. They walk in humility to leave a legacy.

   Who left a legacy for you? Who will follow your example?

3. Our purpose in life is to know Christ and to make him known.

   Ask God for empathy for others and for courage to do lowly tasks that bring glory to God.

CHAPTER 6

Courage to Keep the Marriage Covenant

BY STEVE BUNDY

There is no more lovely, friendly, or charming relationship,
communion, or company, than a good marriage.

MARTIN LUTHER

Sam and Lydia shared the anticipation and excitement of most new parents. When their son Boston was born, Sam felt a pride he'd never before experienced. The joy of those early months with Boston confirmed this young couple's desire for more children, and before long Lydia was expecting—a daughter this time! The months flew by, and soon a sweet little girl was bundled in pink. It was a father's dream come true. The house overflowed with toys, diapers, cribs, and swings. When friends teased Sam about sleepless nights, he just smiled and said, "Fatherhood rocks!" But the good times didn't last long.

Shortly after Sadie was born, Sam and Lydia began to notice that something was different about Boston. Their busy schedule had overshadowed the fact that his speech seemed to be delayed. To their surprise Boston had reached his second birthday without saying a single word. They also observed that he didn't play with his little sister. At first they chalked his behavior up to the fact that he was a boy. And, after all, Sadie was a year younger than him. But they still wondered why Boston never interacted with his sister.

Boston's lack of speech and increased isolation resulted in his growing frustration. Eventually he reached his boiling point and showed signs of outright defiance. No amount of discipline seemed to help. By age three Boston intentionally pulled his sister's hair and drew all over the walls. Lydia, who was exhausted from chasing two children, soon came to her wits' end. She and Sam agreed that it was time to see a developmental specialist. Boston's tests revealed a diagnosis of autism.

No Happily-Ever-After Life

Three years later Sam sat in my office with his head in his hands, weeping over the condition of his family. Sadie was receiving little attention from either parent because Boston's behavior had become a complete mystery. Lydia's fatigue and depression had driven her to seek comfort in the arms of another man. Sam felt broken, embarrassed, and helpless.

Sam and I spent the next several months meeting together to talk and pray. In the beginning he heaped a great deal of blame on Lydia for her infidelity. Eventually, though, Sam admitted that ever since Boston's diagnosis, he had checked out as a husband and father. He had buried himself in his work, claiming it was for the family. Sam had left all the responsibilities of parenting to Lydia: schoolwork, therapy treatments, doctor visits, and the dreaded IEP (Individualized Educational Plan) meetings with teachers and school specialists. Over time Lydia imploded emotionally into a state of self-preservation in order to survive.

In counseling Sam came to a place of repentance for abdicating his role as a husband and father. He set new priorities for his life, putting Christ at the center. He changed jobs to better serve his wife and family. Yet still, after months of trying to repair their marriage, Sam and Lydia divorced. The new lifestyle she had embraced had become her escape from the harsh realities of home. Lydia's heart had hardened toward Sam, and she wanted to start over with a new life.

Sam and Lydia's story is a true one with a sad ending.[1] I share it with you for two reasons. First, family life is not a Hollywood movie in which everyone lives happily ever after. There are consequences for bad choices and sinful behaviors. In the real world families do get hurt. Marriages do fall apart. Children are emotionally and spiritually damaged by divorce, and some scars never mend. Hollywood loves to tell stories that make sexual or emotional escape look appealing, in which the "good" spouse ends up happier with someone else. Unfortunately, those stories fail to portray the aftermath with its long-term emotional and spiritual wounds on both sides of the family.

Second, Sam and Lydia's story illustrates that unfaithfulness in marriage is not limited to the physical realm. While there was no excuse for Lydia's affair, we must recognize that Sam left their marriage emotionally and spiritually long before Lydia left it physically. Simply put, Sam abdicated his role and responsibility as husband, leaving Lydia to fend for herself. When husbands abandon their position in marriage, there are no happy endings.

The Mystery of Marriage

In God's eyes one of the greatest relationships on Earth is between two people in marriage. It is so significant that in Ephesians 5:25–28 marriage is used as an example of our relationship with Christ:

> Husbands, go all out in your love for your wives, exactly as Christ did for the church—a love marked by giving, not

getting. Christ's love makes the church whole. His words evoke her beauty. Everything he does and says is designed to bring the best out of her, dressing her in dazzling white silk, radiant with holiness. And that is how husbands ought to love their wives. They're really doing themselves a favor—since they're already "one" in marriage (*MSG*).

Paul describes the covenant relationship between a man and a woman as the act of them leaving their parents and becoming one flesh. Think about that for a moment. Two people becoming one flesh. It is so mind-blowing that Paul calls it a mystery.[2] This mystical union is consummated in the act of sexual lovemaking, which is one of life's greatest pleasures. It has been explored, examined, and written about since the beginning of mankind—a union so special that the result is nothing short of a miracle: the creation of a new life. A son or a daughter! A family!

So what has gone wrong? Why are so many marriages falling apart, especially when disability is thrust upon a couple? Why does this wonderful union that miraculously unites two people often end in unhappiness and separation?

I wish that I possessed a silver bullet that could target a solution to these issues. When I counseled Sam years ago, we searched for answers to restore his marriage and save his family. But answers to these problems don't come easy. I have yet to discover a one-size-fits-all solution that will fix every marriage. However, what I can share here are some real and practical truths that can help our marriages to survive and, with God's help, to thrive!

God Is for Your Marriage

Marriage was established by God. It is the oldest sacrament recorded in history and is the basis on which God established humanity and family: "For this reason a man will leave his father and mother and be united to his wife, and they will become one flesh" (Genesis 3:24). Throughout the Old and New Testament, marriage is regarded as a sacred, intimate bond between a man and a woman. The tradition of marriage has influenced not only every religion known to man but courts and laws as well. The marriage covenant is so powerful that it requires a minister or a judge, a license, witnesses, and a recorded contract filed for legal verification. And even more important than our legal systems, *God* recognizes our marriages.

In Mark 10 Jesus was confronted with the topic of divorce by the Pharisees, who tried to trap him by asking a trick question. These men of the law knew that God hated divorce but that he also had allowed it in Old Testament times.[3] Jesus explained to them that God made that provision for divorce because men's hearts were hard. He was quick to remind them that marriage was God's idea from the beginning and added this stern warning: "What God has joined together, let man not separate" (Mark 10:9).

It is God's desire to see our marriages thrive. Even in the midst of the challenges of parenting children with special needs, our marriages can still succeed. Many voices in our culture may be screaming another perspective: "Get out!" "Start over!" "You can do better." "You deserve more." "Your marriage was a mistake!" But in reality God has us right where we need to be—married to the bride that he chose for us. The grass is not greener on the other side of the fence; we just don't see all the brown spots from our side.

Satan is not for marriages. Make no mistake—he sets traps for the innocent! His mission is to destroy families, and sometimes he succeeds, leaving single parents to face a mountain of hurt and uncertainty. However, if you've experienced divorce, there is hope for you. It is found in making Jesus Christ your climbing partner. Like my friend Sam discovered, you need Christian brothers who can pull you up and help secure the rope (more about that in chapter

8). Divorce may be one of life's most hurtful tragedies, but as we'll see in the next section, a disability in our family need not be.

A Disability Is Not a Family Tragedy

While some people view having a child with a disability as a family tragedy, that idea could not be further from the truth. Over the years the divorce rate for couples raising children with disabilities has been reported to be 80 percent. This statistic has appeared on websites, been printed in news articles, and discussed on talk shows without sufficient research. Such misinformation can be dangerous, because couples who are expecting a child with a disability could be influenced to consider abortion or adoption without knowing the facts.

Daniel J. Vance, licensed professional counselor at Vernon Center Counseling Services in greater Minneapolis–St. Paul, has done extensive research in this area. In his paper "The Effect of Children with Disabilities on Marital Stability," he discounts these statistics:

> A number of researchers, especially in the last 15 years, have found a wide range of divorce rates among married couples of children with disabilities. These rates often varied significantly, not only study to study, but also according to the type or severity of the disability. They ranged from less than average for parents of a child with Down syndrome to more than two times the average for parents of a child with cerebral palsy, congenital heart disease or blindness. . . . Not one study conclusively showed an average divorce rate in the 75% to 85% range among all children with disabilities.[4]

Vance suggests that pastors and marriage counselors can play an important role in dispelling misconceptions about divorce by encouraging couples to get accurate information about their child's unique needs from their doctors. Some counselors recommend mentoring programs that match young couples with parents who have raised children with similar disabilities. Mentors can shed light on available community services and special education as well as provide needed support throughout the various stages these parents will face in the years ahead.

We can also look to God's Word for wise instructions on how to have a healthy marriage.

- *United hearts and minds.* "My purpose is that they may be encouraged in heart and united in love, so that they may have the full riches of complete understanding, in order that they may know the mystery of God, namely, Christ" (Colossians 2:2).
- *Shared family values.* "These commandments that I give you today are to be upon your hearts. Impress them on your children. Talk about them when you sit at home" (Deuteronomy 6:6–7).
- *Enjoyed sexual intimacies.* "Marriage should be honored by all, and the marriage bed kept pure" (Hebrews 13:4).
- *Promised marriage blessings.* "A wife of noble character . . . is worth far more than rubies. Her husband has full confidence in her and lacks nothing of value" (Proverbs 31:10–11).

To Have and to Hold

I have one of the greatest wives in the world. No, seriously, I definitely married up. Melissa's love and devotion to God, to me, and to our sons is unwavering. She lives sacrificially, and I never question her love for me. She is the most giving person I've ever met—both to our family and to everyone she meets. While our love for one another is strong, we've had to learn how to journey together over twenty-one years of marriage, because at times life gets very difficult. I am grateful for the many people who have spoken truth into our lives and to a wise special counselor who once helped us work through our communication challenges.

Even under the best of circumstances, marriage is a challenge. Two different personalities from diverse backgrounds often struggle to maintain love, harmony, and peace. Introduce a child with disabilities into the mix, and you often find the perfect storm. Couples who commit to loving each other "for better or for worse" can be torn apart when something "worse" than they expected arrives on their doorstep. Tension, friction, and frustration can become daily visitors, and marriages can fall prey to their attacks. Contrary to what some may think, the hardest blow to a marriage does not necessarily come at the point of initial diagnosis of the disability. Rather, like a slow current erodes a river bank, daily stressors take a toll until one or both partners have nothing left to give. In my experience the primary current that erodes most marriages is a breakdown in *communication*.

When my family vacationed in Hawaii, the one stop I didn't want to miss was Pearl Harbor. As a war-history buff, I looked forward to sharing this historical site with my nine-year-old son, Jaron. During the tour I was struck by a single communication-related detail that had taken place between a radar operator and a commander on that historical day that had a profound impact on the attack's outcome. Let me describe it to you exactly as it is recorded at Pearl Harbor:

> At 0700, Privates Joseph P. Lockard and George Elliott detected a large, unusual "target." They called the officer on duty at the Fort Shafter Information Center. First Lieutenant Kermit A. Tyler, a pilot temporarily assigned to the center,

was on his first full day there. "At about 0715 I got a call from Private Joseph Lockard," Tyler recalled. "He said it was the biggest plot he had ever seen. . . . I told him, 'Don't worry about it. It's O.K.'" Tyler had reason to believe they were friendly aircraft. In fact, a flight of B-17s was due to land at Hickam Field at 0800. Tyler later explained, "There was no way of telling what they were. The problem was, (at that hour) we had no identification people on staff."

As you've probably figured out by now, that "plot" on the radar was an image of the Japanese bombers headed to destroy the Pearl Harbor fleet and aircraft. Imagine how events might have been different—if those on duty had responded with a readiness for battle, if they had been alert instead of treating this radar contact as non-threatening, if aircraft had been scrambled, and if Navy ships had been prepared for battle and ordered into open waters. Instead, commanders now admit that this failure in communication remains one of the greatest "what if" questions in the history of Pearl Harbor.

Men, the Bible reminds us to be ready for attack: "Be self-controlled and alert. Your enemy the devil prowls around like a roaring lion looking for someone to devour" (1 Peter 5:8). Like the Japanese bombers coming in stealth mode, our enemy is seeking to destroy our marriages with a surprise attack. And ironically, like what happened at Pearl Harbor, the breakdown that often leads to overwhelming conflict is in our communication. Any effective war plan includes the first rule of battle: confuse or destroy the enemy's communications. Generals know that when communication is taken out, chaos ensues. The same is true in a marriage. Without clear, honest, and consistent communication between spouses, division and destruction can swoop down when we least expect it.

Vows of the Heart

How well do you communicate with your wife? If you're like most men, the word "fine" often describes your feelings and emotions. I understand—I get it! Most evenings after work, Melissa asks, "Honey, how was your day?" I automatically respond with, "Fine," hoping that it will satisfy her (even when I know it won't). Men, we must learn to dig deeper.

We can point out that marriage vows include "to have and to hold" but contain nothing about promising long conversations about our innermost feelings. But face it—God created women with a need for meaningful discussions. A wife needs an open exchange of ideas with her partner, her lover, and the father of her children.

Silence can cause wives to feel abandoned. Nothing—and I mean *nothing*—means more to our wives than to know that as husband and wife, we are in this together! As uncomfortable as it may seem, we must listen with our heart, not just our head, and take time to learn our wife's communication style. Ask your wife, "How would you like me to communicate?" or, "When is a good time for us to talk?" You won't regret this investment in your marriage, because it will pay off in large dividends.

Disability Makes Me Mad

We have met the enemy and he is us!
POGO, A 1950S CARTOON CHARACTER

In addition to the issue of communication, there are two major emotions that most men do not like to deal with: anger and pride. Let's break them down.

Most men do not realize it, but anger is connected to fear. There are two kinds of fear in this world. The first is a God-given fear that protects us from doing stupid things. When I think of this kind of fear, a reality show that mesmerizes my son Jaron comes to mind. It takes place in Texas and focuses on men who make a career of catching rattlesnakes. The only time I watched this show with Jaron, one of the snake catchers was too slow and had to be hospitalized for—you guessed it—a rattlesnake bite! That's what happens when we ignore this common-sense fear that shouts, *"Don't mess with rattlesnakes!"*

The second kind of fear is subtle and not connected to common-sense circumstances. It is the kind of fear that says, "I am not in control of this. Therefore, I don't want to deal with it." This fear can grip a dad's heart when his child receives a disturbing diagnosis, undergoes surgery, or is simply rejected at the playground. We can't fix it, and the unknown creates fear in us. This leads to anxiety that is often expressed in anger. It is difficult for most men to process these feelings, much less for us to communicate them to our wives. A sense of anxiety and inadequacy overtakes us and finds its expression in anger.

The other feeling I mentioned is pride. I don't need to say too much about pride, because the men reading this book have already conquered pride, right? (I hope you're smiling as I am right now.) I have a running joke with my staff. Every now and then, I'll say, "Once I conquered humility, everything else was downhill." We all have a good laugh, and it lightens a sometimes tense conversation around a delicate issue. In truth, every man reading this book, including me, is steeped in pride. It's part of our human makeup, and we struggle with it every day. Pride says, "Something or someone is causing me discomfort without my approval. How dare this or that invade my space!" Oh, we may not articulate it, but it's going on deep inside. Pride says, "I am god of my universe; therefore, do not disrupt my world." It has been around since the evil Lucifer desired to overtake the throne from God and since Adam rebelled in the garden. Pride led King David astray when he had his way with another man's wife. And—no one can escape it!

When fear and anxiety collide with pride, anger creates an unhealthy dynamic in a marriage. Most men are inept at explaining this mixture of emotions, because we see ourselves as knights in shining armor coming to our wives' rescue—not as soul mates to confide in, which is what our wives truly desire.

It helps to remember that the tragedy is the presence of anxiety and fear—not the disability of your child. Anxiety and fear create the tension that leads to a slip of the tongue, cutting words, agitation over small mistakes, and that "I'm fed up" attitude. Eventually, voices get louder, and doors start slamming. Men retreat into themselves (or the television), and women take refuge in their tears. Apologies and flowers may eventually follow, but deep down we desire a healthy way to affirm true love for one another.

I have waged the war with anger and have the battle scars to prove it. I would like to say that I have slain the giant once and for all, but though I have made great progress and won some battles, anger lives to raise its ugly head another day. Early in Caleb's life when I was grappling with his disabilities, I'll admit that I actually destroyed a laptop in anger. I wanted to tell customer service that the laptop was defective, but that was difficult with my shoe print stamped on it and a hammer wedged in the keyboard.

There is no easy answer to managing one's anger, but we can trust the power of the Holy Spirit to lead us into mature and godly responses when angry feelings arise. It is a matter of our surrendering our fear, anxiety, and pride to the Lord, asking his gentle Spirit to lead us. The apostle Paul says,

> Let your gentleness be evident to all. . . . Do not be anxious about anything, but in everything, by prayer and petition, with thanksgiving, present your requests to God. And the peace of God, which transcends all understanding, will guard your hearts and your minds in Christ Jesus (Philippians 4:5–7).

Notice how Paul's words are a pattern for us: "Gentleness. . . prayer. . . thanksgiving. . . peace." If we desire a life of gentleness, we must give all our anxiety and fear to *Jehovah Shalom*, the Lord of Peace. His *peace* goes beyond our limited understanding and is found in God's Son, Jesus, whom the Old Testament prophet Isaiah called a "Wonderful Counselor, Mighty God, Everlasting Father, Prince of Peace" (Isaiah 9:6).

Ken Tada, co-author of *Joni and Ken: An Untold Love Story*, experienced this epiphany of peace during one of his frequent fly-fishing trips. While his love for God and Joni had never wavered through their years together, Ken admits that he underestimated the challenges of being married to a woman with quadriplegia. At times he became increasingly overwhelmed by the unceasing demands of caring for a woman with chronic, extreme pain. He sank into depression that caused him and Joni to drift apart. But God had a special message for Ken three years before Joni's breast cancer in 2010 that would change their marriage forever:

> [Ken] followed a trail to the upper part of the reservoir by the dam and found a wide rock warmed by the summer sunshine. Sitting down, he looked up into the deep vault of wilderness sky and said, "Well, Father, here I am again. Your son Ken Tada. Is there anything you want to say to me?" And this time, to Ken's considerable surprise, there was.
>
> It hadn't been an audible voice, but it was absolutely clear, piercing his thoughts like a sudden shaft of sunlight. And he had no doubt who was speaking.
>
> "Joni is the most precious gift I have given you. You take care of her." . . .
>
> What exactly did God mean?[5]

After Joni's stage-3 breast-cancer diagnosis, Ken began to understand God's message in a new way. The thought of losing his wife to cancer changed everything, making quadriplegia seem like a minor issue. This time Ken jumped right in with both feet and took over his wife's care, staying by her side throughout surgery, tests, and months of chemotherapy.

> Ken remembered the words the Lord had spoken to him in Montana as he sat on the rock in the sunshine by the dam. "Joni is the most precious gift I have given you. Take care of her!" Now he realized what that had been all about. God had been preparing him, getting him ready, calling him into a deeper, stronger, closer walk with himself.[6]

Because Ken took a deliberate step of faith to get alone with God and to seek godly wisdom, he found courage to care for his wife and to renew his marriage covenant.

God Heals Hurting Marriages

Dave Elsinger, Equip project manager of the Evangelical Free Church in Fullerton, California, wondered how his marriage could survive one child with autism. Then his second child was diagnosed with the same condition:

> Our son, Stephen, was born while we were missionaries in Ukraine, where there were few options for children with autism. Soon after our return to the U.S., our daughter Elizabeth was born. At twelve months old, she stopped smiling and responding to her name. This was especially hard on my wife, Oksana, who grew up in the Soviet Union. We cried out to the Lord and to our church family for help.
> The stress of having two children diagnosed with a developmental disorder drove us to seek Christian counseling. Our individual differences and marital expectations became very heavy. I

did not expect marriage and family to be struggle-free, but I had dreamed of having a "normal" family life like the one I enjoyed growing up. From what I read about families with special needs kids, they had anything but a normal life. Many couples with a child on the autism spectrum were struggling or dissolved under the pressure. Even with counseling, church friends, and help from therapists and county social workers, we too struggled greatly. More than once I felt like I couldn't handle what God had given us. I was angry at my wife for her lack of respect, and the distance between us grew. I knew that she was also hurting and just as confused about what was next for us as a couple and for our family. I complained to the Lord about what seemed to be a no-win situation. We both feared that we would end up being full-time therapists for two children who might never be able to care for themselves. This is not what we bargained for when we said, "I do."

I can't explain exactly why I chose to hold on to the Lord and His word. Psalm 46:1–7 became an anchor promise that I clung to each day: "God is our refuge and strength, an ever-present help in trouble." I chose to believe that God was with me, watching over my children and marriage. Through the love of God's people, we were upheld even in the waves of doubt. With prayer and therapy, our daughter Elizabeth improved, overcoming her autism diagnosis. Stephen also made good progress through ongoing therapy, love, and prayer. We continue to learn about the way God has designed him and are thankful for his incredible gifts. When Stephen was age 4, he began playing the piano by ear, and at age 6 began taking formal lessons and composing his own music.

Our marriage became stronger as we chose to hold on to God's promises, give each other breaks, and spend time together with the help of family and friends. We chose to love each other out of the strength that God gives us. I exchanged my "dreams" for his plan, which has been more deep and satisfying. Two years ago we had the opportunity to return to the Ukraine in order to help families facing similar struggles but without many of the resources available in the U.S. We have come full circle as a couple and learned to "be still and know" that he is God (Psalm 46:10).

Consider the three things that helped Dave and his wife keep their marriage healthy: (1) holding on to God's promises, (2) giving each other a break, and (3) spending time together with the help of family and friends.

At Joni and Friends we encourage couples to follow this model by hosting Family Retreats across the U.S., by producing inspiring Joni and Friends television episodes, and by helping churches offer respite programs. Family Retreats provide a dynamic week at a beautiful Christian camp that refreshes and strengthens the whole family.[7] Couples and single parents learn to trust and appreciate the short-term missionaries who are assigned to care for their children. Special features at the retreat include dressy dinners and dances, spas, hikes, and support groups.

"At Family Retreat, our family finds strength," say Rico and Karen, whose teenage daughter has multiple disabilities. "When we're at the end of our rope," Rico explains, "Family Retreat sustains us. It also gives us hope for our daughter. For a whole week her disabilities and wheelchair do not prevent her from being involved or loved. She is not on the outside looking in. And the week brings our family closer to God. He has opened my own heart, so I am able to let go and receive his grace."

Every Family Retreat has a camp pastor, who is often the father of a child with a disability. Pastor Jim has been serving at retreats for eight years. He ministers God's light to other families living with disabilities. He knows firsthand the weight and unrelenting demands of disabilities. Jim also understands the overwhelming exhaustion that couples endure. He talks about the power of God to restore joy and peace and to bring fresh power and comfort to marriages. After all that his family has been through, Jim is happy to share with hurting couples the comfort that he himself has received from Family Retreats.

The purpose of a church respite program[8] is to give moms and dads a break from parenting and an opportunity to connect by doing things together such as date nights, shopping, walking in the park, or just resting. Respite events may be offered weekly or bimonthly, for half or whole days. For example, Jill's House provides overnight and weekend respite for children with intellectual disabilities and their families in the greater Washington, D.C. area. This outreach was the vision of Lon and Brenda Solomon, whose daughter Jill has suffered thousands of seizures that have profoundly damaged her brain and left her severely disabled. It is their hope that Jill's House can become a model that will change the way communities address the issues of families and children with special needs.[9]

"Jill's disability has been a defining moment for me as a father and a husband," says Reverend Solomon. "Today, Brenda and I have a much stronger marriage. And Jill has made me a better pastor, providing me the foresight to want to help others with disabilities."[10] While Jim and Brenda will need to care for Jill the rest of their lives, they don't see it as a burden but rather as a privilege.

Ways to Keep Covenant

As creativity goes, sometimes we men need help. So here are a few tips for building a healthy marriage. This list is neither intended as a "guilty list", nor as a "do list" for checking off items. As you prayerfully consider ways to strengthen your marriage, perhaps one or more of these ideas will provide some creative thoughts:

- *Plan a date night.* Yes, I said *plan* something! Knock your wife's socks off by reserving a special night for the two of you. Put time into it as if you were planning a fishing day, a football game, or a business trip. Melissa and I make it a regular habit to have date nights to spend time together without the stresses of home life. And yes, I occasionally make all the plans.
- *Plan a weekend away.* This one is a little more challenging due to childcare. However, if you're able, planning a couple's weekend away can help you both relax, decompress, and enjoy one another's company. If your wife worries about the kids overnight, then plan something close to home so she'll be comfortable knowing that she is just moments away if needed.
- *Pray together.* No, I am not talking about every morning between children's crying, diaper changing, and lunch making. I tried that road, and trust me, it doesn't work. Find a time that works for both of you and then make it a quality time. Melissa and I find that the best time for us is Saturday mornings.
- *Attend a marriage seminar or Bible study.* Many churches offer small groups that are geared toward marriage growth or have an annual marriage conference that couples can attend together. Melissa and I have benefited over the years by attending such conferences that help us discuss marriage and parenting issues in a safe and Christian context.
- *Be romantic.* No, I did not say have more sex. Our wives see romance in a different light than we do. We tend to think primarily of the physical. Women focus on romantic attitudes, gestures, words, and kind acts that communicate that they are cherished and loved. Treat

your wife like this, and you'll find that you will enjoy this definition of romance as well.

- *Have fun.* This one sounds easy, but our lives are so filled with day-to-day stressors that we can develop negative patterns of interacting with our problems. Remember back when you two were dating and got together to just have fun. You didn't have a care in the world (okay, that may be a little unrealistic), or at least you had fewer problems. You focused on one another and enjoyed simple things. Make the effort to stop thinking about the future and enjoy the journey along the way.

A Promise to Keep

On difficult days I often recall standing at the U.S.S. Arizona Memorial in Pearl Harbor and watching the graphic video depicting the attack. I bring to mind the pictures of the human carnage and twisted metal, where brave men and women fell. I hear the commander's final words regarding the misread radar signal: "Ordinary men placed in extraordinary circumstances; they performed their duty as expected." What Pearl Harbor needed was men who were willing to perform beyond the ordinary when the circumstances called for extraordinary.

I will never forget that day, because, like Ken Tada, I experienced God speaking to my spirit. He called me to a higher commitment than I had known before, as I uttered a humble prayer:

God, don't let me be an ordinary man, an ordinary husband, or an ordinary father. Help me perform as a man of God in a way that rises to the challenge of my extraordinary circumstances.

Are you facing some extraordinary circumstance in your marriage? Is there a battle going on in your family since God brought a child with special needs into your home? If so, God is calling you to keep your marriage covenant. With his help you can do it. Your son or daughter deserves a father who lives above the ordinary.

GROWTH STEPS

1. God designed marriage to be a sacred union between you and your wife.

   How are you following God's instructions to successfully participate in his design?

2. God asks you to love your wife in a way that brings out her best qualities.

   What virtues have you learned to cherish most about your wife? How would she answer that question about you?

3. Men of courage keep their promises.

   In the hard times, who or what brings you peace and helps you remain faithful?

Read 1 Corinthians 13:4-13 with your wife and pray together for strength to trust God.

CHAPTER 7

Courage to Raise Godly Siblings

BY STEVE BUNDY

A child's glory is his father.
PROVERBS 17:6, TLB

It doesn't take a new father long to figure out that children do not come with instruction manuals. Fatherhood is a lifelong journey of trial and error. Men by nature are simply not wired with the same nurturing instincts that mothers are. Even Hollywood has figured this out. It's why movies like *Jingle All the Way*, starring Arnold Schwarzenegger and Sinbad, resonate with dads. In this film Howard Langston (played by Schwarzenegger) is an absent father who seems to always fumble his way through parenting, not quite sure how to connect with his son. Then, Howard learns that his son is infatuated with the hottest toy on the market, Turbo Man. It is the one toy his son *must have* for Christmas. Sadly, Howard finds this out on Christmas Eve, and shopping time is running out. Maybe you recall the scene: he finally finds a toy store with one Turbo Man left. Spying the toy, Howard makes a huge lunge for it. The scene becomes a destructive, comical battle between Howard and his rival, postal worker Myron Larabee (played by Sinbad).

127

As funny as this story is to watch, there is a grain of truth in real-life Christmas sell-outs for toys like Cabbage Patch Kids® and Mighty Morphin Power Rangers. As parents attempting to connect with our kids, we sometimes fall prey to the "buy their approval" culture. This mindset also displays the challenges that fathers have connecting with their children—challenges that can increase when a disability is mixed in and a father's time becomes more divided. Few men have had the luxury of growing up with an ideal father figure who modeled the biblical principles of parenting. In fact, many men have had no fatherly role model whatsoever in their lives. It's one of the reasons that we felt compelled to include this chapter. We can all admit that fathers do not have everything figured out, and we can always use some encouragement and direction along the way.

In this chapter we'll hear from brothers and sisters of siblings with disabilities. They are often the ones who feel overshadowed by the requirements of the child with special needs. These siblings have the same desires as the child with special needs for attention, support, love, and respect, which parents must consider. They also have strong opinions, some positive, others—not so much. Regardless, their feelings and thoughts are valid, and they have a lot to teach us dads! It's important to keep two facts in mind:

1. Perfect fathers don't exist.
2. You're not a father by accident.

Your children were not drawn out of a hat and placed in your home in some kind of cosmic lottery. A holy God with infinite wisdom selected each child's gender, temperament, and interest knowing ahead of time how each one would help you become a better man. Every parent at one time or another asks, "Why in the world did God give *me* children?" I've got the answer for you—because God loves you and wants you to become more like his Son, Jesus Christ.

It's been said that the best way to teach character is to have it around the house. The following quotes are from siblings who have had various experiences, many of which your own children will also experience growing up in your family. As a courageous father, you have an opportunity to train up your children to find and follow God's plan for their lives.[1] Or as theologian C. H. Spurgeon once said, "Train your child in the way you know you should have gone yourself."

Siblings Need to Be Heard

We never got to do normal things like going out to dinner or sporting events. We always had to worry about how my brother would act.—Joshua, age 10

We are a close family. We all are involved with Special Olympics, which has had a big impact on my brother's disability.—Libby, age 13

I worry a lot about what will happen when my parents die and somewhat resent that I will be the primary caregiver . . . which I'm ashamed about.—Jake, age 16

> Dad's response:
> "Talk to me—I'll listen!"

Growing up with a sibling who has special needs creates a childhood experience that is sometimes hard to fully understand. Dr. Mark Baker, executive director of the La Vie Christian Counseling Centers, has a sibling with disabilities and now counsels others as a clinical psychologist. Dr. Baker says, "Witnessing the suffering of a brother or sister brings its own kind of suffering. The pain, confusion, embarrassment, and sense of responsibility that comes from being the 'normal' sibling can have emotional consequences that last a lifetime. It is important for family members to create a healthy dialog in which children can articulate their pain. In wrestling with the issues, children can learn to not only survive, but to thrive as they mature."

Children will often have the same fears, anxieties, and concerns that parents have. In fact, these emotions may actually be magnified, because siblings realize that someday their brother or sister may be their sole responsibility. These concerns can have many sentiments attached to them, including guilt and shame. Or siblings may have questions they're afraid to ask, such as:

- Do my parents love me as much as my sibling?
- Why are my parents so cranky and stressed out?
- How can my friends understand me?
- Why do I feel so angry and lonely?
- When will our family get back to normal?

It is important that we allow our children to openly discuss their true feelings. This is never easy, especially with boys. Girls tend to be more talkative by nature than boys do. Dr. James Dobson, founder of Focus on the Family and Family Talk, says, "Opportunities for meaningful communication between fathers and sons must be created. And it's work to achieve."[2] These words struck home with me when my son Jaron was only seven years old. His brother Caleb's behaviors were becoming more intrusive at times due to his autism, and he was increasingly the center of attention in our home. But I had no idea that at such an early age, Jaron would absorb this environment and wrestle with its realities.

One day while getting ready for school, Jaron began to cry. This continued for several days in a row. I must confess that I became somewhat irritated with him. We were already dealing with Caleb's cries and screams, and I didn't want to handle another behavioral issue. I resorted to the typical "man up" mentality and declared that we were leaving on time whether he was crying or not. With this—his crying increased! It was not just in the mornings but during some afternoons as well.

After several weeks of this pattern and with seemingly no obvious solution, Pat Verbal, a good friend of mine and a significant contributor to this book, gave me a simple piece of advice. She said, "Have you talked with him about his feelings regarding Caleb? He is at an age at which self-awareness is kicking in, and he may be struggling with the reality of his disabled brother." This had not occurred to me. The next day I cleared my schedule to take Jaron out for ice cream and to spend time talking with him. I took off work a little early to pick Jaron up from school. We started out with small talk. I asked him how it was going, and he responded that things were fine. We consumed our treat and enjoyed conversations about his favorite sports.

After the ice cream we got back into my car, where I turned the conversation to the challenges that come with Caleb's disability. I shared that I had struggled at times to accept the way that God had created Caleb. I opened up to my young son about how I had had to work through my own anger and that I still dealt with it at times. I admitted that I sometimes felt embarrassed by Caleb's outbursts and tantrums when our family was in public. Jaron listened quietly, but I knew that he was absorbing everything he heard. Then I looked at him and said, "You know son, it's okay to have those feelings. Feelings are not right or wrong; they just exist. It's what we do with those feelings that matters. We can hold them in and feel guilty, or we can talk about them. I am here for you, and you can tell me anything, especially your feelings about Caleb."

I could plainly see the relief in my son's countenance. It was as if I had taken a huge boulder off his chest, and he could come up for air. He burst into tears; guilt and shame were washed away as he expressed his desire for a "normal" brother. As deeply as he loved Caleb, he wished he would not hit, kick, and scream in public. He shared some of the fears about Caleb's future. It was all locked away in his little seven-year-old brain. We talked for some time, and as we did, I constantly reassured him that his feelings were okay, that I understood.

That day marked a transition not only in Jaron's life but in mine too. Jaron stopped crying, and I truly believe that he came to a greater peace about his brother. I realized that we cannot ignore the very real fears and emotions that siblings will encounter on this journey called disability. As hard as we try as parents to shield our other children from some of the raw feelings that come with disability or try to help them focus on the positive, the truth is that they need to be able to express their emotions and feel heard. Brothers and sisters are as much a part of the family's journey as we parents are. In fact, they may need to be heard more than anyone else. Today, I can honestly say that Jaron is the greatest son any father could ask for and a caring sibling to his brother. I am thankful God slowed me down for Jaron to be heard.

Siblings Need to Know That They Are Valued

> My sister's autism is the biggest tragedy of my life. I hated being made fun of as a kid. I love my sister, but it has been painful for my whole family to see her robbed of her ability to communicate.
> —Heather, age 17

> Through my sister, I've learned tolerance, patience, and to be thankful for all that I have. I'm less self-conscious and more accepting of people outside the "norm."—Charlie, age 21

> **Dad's response:**
> **"Show me your heart—I see you!"**

The Bible tells us that God knows our thoughts before we even think them.[3] So he definitely understands when our children feel less "special" than their special-needs brothers or sisters. Many siblings say that they feel invisible at times, yet they can become very good at hiding their emotions. As an earthly father, ask God to help you recognize moments when siblings may be struggling with their own identity and place in the family. These are teachable moments when they need the assurance that you see them and that God sees them too.

Courtney grew up sandwiched between two brothers with disabilities. Their disability classifications include pervasive developmental disability not otherwise specified (PDD-NOS), bipolar disorder, and seizure disorder. One of her earliest memories is of being at her family's cabin by the lake. Her parents had their hands full with her energetic eight-year-old brother and her newborn baby brother. They didn't notice that their bubbly three-year old daughter was racing to the end of the boat dock to see the pretty flowers. They didn't see her fall into the water or hear her soft cry as she sank lower into the water, weighted down by her shoes and sundress. Courtney recalls trying desperately to breathe, but her mouth was filling up with water. Thankfully, one of her dad's friends jumped into the lake and pulled Courtney out. In retelling the story her parents often joked about it, saying, "Who was watching little Courtney?" Unfortunately, this incident was a symbolic point in her life that would take her years to overcome.

One woman in the Bible called out to God as *El Roi*, The God Who Sees Me. As the servant of Sarah, Hagar was obedient in becoming Abraham's mistress and bearing him a son. But Sarah's jealousy drove Hagar and her son away and into the middle of the desert, where she felt completely alone—until she realized that God was with her—that God saw her![4]

Do you see each of your children as unique individuals with their own personality, gifts, learning style, and interests? Have you told them that they can't hide from God or pretend they are okay when they're not because *El Roi* sees them and cares about everything that concerns them?

Most of my personal stories in this book have related my experiences as a father. Now I want to share my experience as a sibling. My brother is now forty-six years old. He was born at a time when diagnoses of mental disorders were not as common as they are today. Unfortunately, there was little available then to parents for clinical therapy, much less any in-home therapies. I did not understand what was happening with my brother throughout most of my childhood. All I knew was that he was different from other kids and made home life very difficult for my parents—and for me.

It was many years before titles were attached to my brother's behaviors and treatment became available. Today, he is much healthier and I am proud of his achievements. I do not have his permission to go into great detail about his diagnosis, but suffice it to say that both he and my parents did the best that they could, considering the resources they had to work with. In fact, my parents, who were teenagers themselves when they became parents, did a great job of keeping our family together.

As an adult, I've been blessed to discover that we often learn from past experience when we have the chance to reflect upon our journey. Such reflection came to me when I was in graduate school. I took a class titled "The Inner Life of the Leader." It focused on helping students have a better self-awareness, which is important to becoming a better leader. One assignment was to characterize our family life at age fourteen by placing other students in statue-like positions to resemble each member of our family. For example, if one's mother was primarily a homemaker, a student might be positioned as a statue cooking in a kitchen—you get the idea. We had several weeks' notice before the in-class demonstration was due. My week came, and I positioned students in certain positions to reflect my family's makeup when I was fourteen.

The first student I positioned in the center of the group. He was focused on himself and throwing a tantrum at the same time. That member of the family was my brother. The second student I positioned close to my brother, with her hands grabbing at her hair and a sense of despair on her face. That member was my mother, whose emotions and energy were consumed by my brother. The third student I positioned further away and looking away, with a hammer and nail in his hand. This represented my dad, who dealt with my brother's chaos by pouring himself into his construction work. He was turned away from the family, because he was an absent father. Finally, I positioned the last student the furthest away from everyone. His face was looking at his father, but his body was going the opposite direction, away from everyone. That member was me.

I was not prepared for the emotions this assignment stirred in me as I commented on each family member. I was very emotional when talking about my own position, because I was so connected to my father. That may seem obvious from my previous explanation of my brother's tremendous emotional issues and how absorbed my mom was with his needs. The statues showed that I did not get the attention from my mom that I wished I'd had. Her hands were full with handling my brother.

Now that I'm raising a son with special needs, I better understand what my mom went through, and I am glad to report that she and I have a great relationship today.

While every boy wants his mom's attention, he receives his self-identity from his father. I positioned the student's face representing me looking toward my father, because I desperately wanted my father's attention and approval. I wanted to know that he was proud of me. More than that, I needed to know that I measured up in his eyes. I needed to know who I was and that he saw me for who I was. My body was positioned away from the family because I did not receive what I was longing for from my dad. Therefore, I spent a great deal of time alone—away from the entire family. It was the easiest way for me to cope with the dysfunction.

The other reason I was so emotional in class was because I gave this demonstration two years after my father passed away. I am glad to say that before his death I had several wonderful years of connecting with my dad, mostly while bass fishing. I think he realized that time was passing by and we could not recapture the past but that we could make some great memories in the present. I'm not sure I ever fully received what I was looking for from my dad, but one thing I know for sure is that he saw me.

From personal experience as a sibling who felt overshadowed, I can tell you this:

"Dads, you must show children how much they are highly valued in your eyes." They must know that you will not overlook them. Show them that nothing is more important to you than your relationship with them. They need to know that you see them for who they truly are in the family!

Siblings Need a Godly Example

I'm convinced that there is no greater example a father can give his children than a bent knee before God. Our children will see us in every situation in life. They watch us do life in real time with our joys, fears, successes, and failures. Unfortunately, we don't get the luxury of practicing for every circumstance that comes our way. Sometimes we'll react to situations, and more often than we'd like to admit, we won't measure up to the men of God we hope to be. So it's important to teach our children by example to depend upon Almighty God. They need to know that it's okay to need a Savior. Despite what our culture tries to tell us, our strengths are found in our weaknesses.[5]

Dad's response:
"Watch me—I can help!"

Reverend Bob Bjerkaas, pastor of the Church in the Canyon in Calabasas, California, has four children, including one with a disability. His son has multiple handicapping conditions that make life challenging at times. One such occasion had to do with some bullies at his son's school. As Bob tells the story:

There is a passage in James 1:19 that reminds us to put away all anger because anger does not accomplish the righteousness of God. As a man, I understand how men think. I know that for better or worse, men often see something happen that's not right, and it naturally makes us angry.

It happened to me once over my son's neurological challenges. He has epilepsy and a severe tic disorder which causes repetitive behaviors and an obsession with flapping his hands. He also has verbal guttural sounds where certain unnecessary syllables are interjected into words or rapid eye movements that are uncontrollable. We all know, especially those of us who remember our childhood, that kids can be fairly cruel to other kids.

It is my habit after work every day to track down each one of my children and to tell them I love them and missed them. Then, I ask about their day. The kids often respond with a generic "okay," but one day my son said, "It was the worst day ever!" For him, that is not uncommon. It's amazing how many "worst days ever" children can have, but in talking to him further, I discovered that he was being teased by some bullies at school. As his dad, I started getting very angry. I felt my blood begin to boil, and before long I saw the color red. My first impulse was to track down the parents of those kids who had ruined my son's day and set them straight. Then, I immediately noticed that my son was starting to reflect my attitude.

My child was getting angry, too, and it gave me pause. I sensed God's nudging in what was for me an "aha!" moment. My son did not need to get mad nor see me get angry, or even worse to hear me talk about getting even. What he truly needed was to learn to direct his lament back to God. As a father, I knew how important it was to act in righteous ways to defend my children and protect them. Yet, I had to model it before my children by turning my grieved face to the Almighty in the midst of suffering and the effects of fallenness. David said it well in Psalm 77:2, "When I was in distress, I sought the Lord."

Family means so much to me that I have to come alongside my children and weep with them when they have a bad day. I can share with them that God is not pleased when we become angry at the kids on the playground, because anger is counterproductive. It's isolating, and it's arrogant.

Today, living this side of heaven, we trust in the God who performs miracles and promises to display his power among the people.[6]

Bob's first reaction was that of any father—to step in and defend. But Bob also had an opportunity to model to his children the strength of the Lord and not strength in himself. I have not talked with Bob's children about this situation, but I can assure you it will serve as an example to them for the rest of their lives.

T.A.G. – You're It!

I think my father had a harder time accepting my brother's disability. It has caused me to gain so much more respect for my dad—seeing how he really rose to the challenge of my brother and has done so with so much love.—Daniel, age 28

My parents were worried about my having kids. I'm not! It never even crossed my mind.—Susan, age 28

I definitely feel more responsible compared to my friends. I grew up faster. But I want to become a teacher to help children who learn differently, like my brother.—Brittney, age 9

Remember playing tag? I do! It was fun as a child and later with my own kids. One day when Jaron was about age two, he and I were running through the house, trying to hide to avoid being tagged by each other. I dragged the game out a little by pretending not to see Jaron, even when he hid in an obvious spot. I passed him several times until he finally jumped out with a sheepish grin and yelled, "I'm right here!" That's when it hit me: he wanted to be caught. His goal in playing the game was not to get away but to get captured and end up in the arms of his dad. He liked rolling on the floor, being tickled, and knowing that he belonged.

As kids grow up, tag becomes a thing of the past, with one exception—in their heart of hearts children still want to be caught. They want to know that we desperately care about them and will never let anything come between us and them. But keeping kids close won't happen by accident. We need a plan. I'd like to suggest three action steps using the acronym T.A.G. to discuss some tried and true principles of fatherhood: time, assurance and guidance.

Before I do this, let me add this little caveat. If you've sweated through this chapter thinking that you've already blown it as a dad, let me assure you that it's never too late (or too early) to work on an authentic relationship with your child. Perhaps your children are young, and you realize that this season will not last forever. Take advantage of it! Or maybe your children are grown, and you wish you had picked up a book like this years before. And you're wondering how to move forward. Be encouraged! Growth and healing are always possible with any relationship—even as it was with my own dad later in our lives.

Time

It has been said that if you want to see what someone values, look at that person's checkbook and calendar. The evidence will speak for itself. As fathers, we must be intentional about how we plan our time. I confess that I am a recovering "planning addict." If there is a planning tool that has been created, I've used it. Remember the FranklinCovey Planner? I went through three of them. When Microsoft Outlook appeared, I was all over it. When the Palm was released to sync with Outlook, I was in planning heaven. Blackberry? You caught me! Now I'm in the cloud.

One thing our calendars cannot do is prioritize our time. Calendars simply respond to the data that we input. Our children come to understand where they are on our priority list based on the time we spend with them. I'm going to step out on a limb here to refute another popular idea that I disagree with: "It's not the quantity of time that matters; it's the quality of time." I used that saying (or excuse) for years when it came to family time. However, can you imagine showing up one day at work and your boss says to you, "Where have you been? I haven't seen you for the last three days?" To which you respond, "That's okay! It's not the quantity of time I spend at work but the quality of time, right? I'm all yours today." Consequence: unemployment.

In many vocations the needs of the organization are never fully met. This is especially true in ministry. One year I traveled so much that I was literally gone for over two months of the year—not to mention that I took work home on the weekends. Yes, jobs are important! But the first ministry God gave fathers is to our families.

One day as I was leaving for a trip and saying goodbye to Jaron, he told me that it was fine for me to go because helping people was important. I felt so proud of him (and myself). That feeling would have remained had Jaron not kept talking. He added that he was never going to be in the ministry. When I asked him why, he said, "Because you don't get to spend time with your family." That one hurt, but it needed to. I still travel for the ministry, but it is now on a more balanced schedule.

Now don't get me wrong. I understand that our time is divided and that we each fulfill different roles and responsibilities. My challenge to fathers is simple: *Are you intentionally spending quantity* and *quality time with your children? What can you realistically do that you are not doing?*

If we're honest, we can all probably find times in our work schedules that allow us to get home a little earlier. There are weekends when we can watch a little less football or spend less time surfing the Web. If you're a planning addict, like me, actually plan time with your kids. Avoid becoming too rigid, and carve out time just for them.

Assurance

Children need constant reminders that they're not accidents but rather the divine handiwork of God.[7] In the media children are bombarded with messages that their value is connected to their appearance and performance. In the school systems students are taught that they evolved from amoeba by circumstances of chance. Through it all kids will look to their parents for confirmation of who they are and why they exist. As fathers, we need to assure our children that God has a plan for them and that they are fearfully and wonderfully made by him.[8]

At the same time, children need assurance that we accept them and will love them no matter what they are going through at a given moment. Despite how frustrating some of those seasons will be (just think back to your teen years and your parents), our kids rely upon our steadfast love and assurance. Their tough moments will include their sometimes awkward and rude emotions about their brother or sister with special needs. We must walk with them through those emotions to provide guidance and to help them recognize the hand of God in the midst of their daily lives.

Children need to be assured that their sibling with a disability was created in the image of God. God has a plan for their lives just as he does for every person. Exodus 4:11 makes clear that it is God who has created or at some point allowed disabilities to enter into a person's life. His thoughts are not our thoughts, and his ways are not our ways.[9] We may not fully grasp God's plan for disability this side of heaven, but we can help our children understand that God uses every life and works out disability for our good.[10]

Guidance

Children look to parents for guidance. In truth, family members often seek a father's advice. In fact, the principles of leading our family are so important to God that he required them as criteria for church leadership. In 1 Timothy 3:2–7 the apostle Paul lists the qualifications of leadership in the Christian community, saying that fathers must manage their families well. The word "manage" in this verse is not the same term as we use when supervising people at work. It is a word used throughout Scripture to communicate caring as a shepherd cares for his sheep. In other words, we need to guide our family through the challenges of life as a shepherd would guide his sheep. We already discussed several aspects of this, but here are several recommendations to focus on as a father:

- *Prayer.* Lead by example. Be quick to honor God through the act of prayer. Show your family that you lean into God for your own guidance. If you do not already do so, establish a regular prayer time with your wife and children.

This does not have to be exhaustive, but consistency is good. I pray with my boys every night at bedtime.

- *Scripture.* Be a man of the Bible, and teach your children the Scriptures. Psalm 119:105 encourages us, "Your word is a lamp to my feet and a light for my path." There will be many days when your children experience confusion and moral challenges. It is your job to teach them to turn to God's Word for guidance.11 As a captain relies on his compass to point north in the raging seas, so we must teach our children to rely upon the promises of God for guidance when life becomes turbulent.
- *Relationships.* Model healthy relationships. Keep in mind that your children will pattern much of their lifelong relationships based on your example. In case you've never considered this, read 1 Corinthians 15:33: "Bad company corrupts good character." No, that isn't an old wives' tale, it is true. Encourage healthy and godly relationships, which can include regular Christian fellowship by which your family can grow spiritually. It also includes social relationships with coworkers and neighbors in your community. More than once I've cut off a friendship because I felt it was a negative influence on my children. I appreciated those friends, but when their conduct did not line up with what they professed, they were gone—and I don't miss them one bit.

I encourage you to reflect on these T.A.G. points. You'll never regret placing priority on those who look to you for time, assurance, and guidance.

Turbo Man Triumphs

If you've seen that movie *Jingle All the Way*, you may recall its dramatic ending. The two fathers continue to battle it out, trying to secure the precious last Turbo Man doll to make their children's Christmas wishes come true. Howard (Schwarzenegger) stumbles into a parade, where he is mistakenly outfitted with a superhero costume of—you guessed it—Turbo Man and is given the task of giving away one of the coveted dolls. Donning the suit, Howard is the hero of the town parade and presents the Turbo Man doll to his son, Jamie, who is awestruck! But before Jamie can celebrate his new toy, more drama ensues. Turbo Man (Howard) saves the day, of course, and when the suit comes off and Jamie realizes that it is actually his father who has rescued him, he announces that he no longer needs the toy since his father is the real Turbo Man. And everyone lives happily ever after!

In real life dads don't usually get to save the day. But the good news is that a hero suit is not required in order to be a connected father. The principles I've shared in this chapter will go a long way toward assuring each of your children that they hold a special place in your heart. To build a family dynamic in which all our children feel understood, loved and appreciated—now *that* is mission accomplished.

GROWTH STEPS

1. God knows his children, and they know his voice.

   What helps your children enjoy spending time with their dad? How do you create teachable moments?

2. God designed your family and has a perfect plan for each child in your family.

   How are you helping your children know God and find his plan for their lives?

3. Read Deuteronomy 6:4-9.

   Using this passage, consider some ways that you can spend more quality time with your children.

Spend time in prayer, committing each of your children to God. Ask for wisdom to see their hurts and brokenness. Believe God for wisdom to be the Christian father your children deserve.

CHAPTER 8

Courage to Stand as Brothers

BY STEVE BUNDY

God did not write solo parts for very many of us.
He expects us to be participants in the great symphony of life.
DONALD TIPPETT

I recently attended a men's retreat with some guys I meet with regularly for prayer and encouragement. The second night we were there, we gathered in front of the television to watch a movie. At first I thought it was a lame idea—we only go on retreat once a year, so why spend time watching movies? To my surprise the movie was *Act of Valor.* It's a story about U.S. Navy Seals and their military exploits around the world. Suddenly the movie had my full attention, and I was ready for popcorn.

The film revolves around a letter written from a Navy Seal commander to the son of a fallen Seal, telling the boy about the courage, commitment, and honor of his father. The fallen Seal, through an act of heroism, had given his life for his comrades by throwing himself on a grenade. The movie is filled with emotional highs and lows, victories and defeats, as it depicts the incredible bond that Navy Seals have with each of their team members and their families. Scenes move from high adrenaline, life-threatening, top-secret missions to families gathered on the beach enjoying a moment when everyone is safe and out of harm's way.

One particular scene from this movie stayed with me. It's the night before the Seals leave for a mission, and they're gathered with their families. As the commander addresses the Seals, he reminds them of the importance of taking care of things at home. He says, "Everything back home needs to be in balance. I mean, if things aren't right with the family, if things aren't right with the finances, or something's off, it'll pull us all out of balance. If somebody's got an issue, bring it up—everybody's got each other's back." These men know that they need each other; there are no lone rangers in war. They are a band of brothers.

That scene impacts me because it truly captures what I believe happens when fathers of children with special needs connect. They too are like a band of brothers. We may not be in life-threatening situations every day as Navy Seals are, but we often live in life-altering situations in which it can feel as if there are land mines and artilleries raining down on us. I have seen this band-of-brothers camaraderie and experienced it in different settings when fathers are together. It doesn't take much time for the walls to start coming down so that needs can be made known and assurances granted. Comments such as "How can I help?" "What do you need?" "I am here for you!" become the norm. In essence, men begin to know that other men have their backs. Though we might not like to admit it, men don't want to do this thing called fatherhood alone.

Logjams to Friendship

When fathers of children with special needs were asked to identify their number one struggle, the common answer was, "Isolation."

"They feel like they're the only person in the world going through this, which is so irrational," says Greg Schell, director of the Washington State Fathers Network and the dad of a daughter with Down syndrome. "Thousands of people are born with disabilities every year, and they all have a dad." Shell believes that the problem is that men become socialized very differently than women, which often leaves men less prepared to handle a son's or daughter's disability.[1]

Another logjam to building strong, solid friendships can be our lack of communication skills, which we discussed in the previous chapter. This tactic of the enemy works to isolate us from our wives and children as well as from male friends. And it exposes our lives to even greater attacks such as addictions, abuse, depression, and hopelessness. There is a good reason why Peter describes the enemy as a lion: "Your enemy the devil prowls around like a roaring lion looking for someone to devour" (1 Peter 5:8). A lion's natural instinct is to disperse a herd of goats or sheep so that one becomes separated from the rest, isolated, and vulnerable to attack. The result is certain death for the animal and a warm dinner for the lion!

Thankfully, Scripture doesn't leave us without hope, like unprotected sheep. Peter reminds us that there is strength in the brotherhood: "Resist him [the devil], standing firm in the faith, because you know that your brothers throughout the world are undergoing the same kind of sufferings" (1 Peter 5:9). He continues in that chapter to speak of friends who have supported him in times of need, such as Silas, a faithful brother, those in the church at Babylon, and his son in the Lord, Mark.

A man's natural reaction to feelings of isolation and vulnerability can prompt him to further withdraw from others. We rationalize like this: *Don't talk about the issues, and perhaps they'll go away.* Thus, we pull back into a self-centered mode of handling life on our own. I've tried it and can honestly tell you that it doesn't work very well, nor does it bring glory to God.

Busting up life's logjams requires the help of friends and brothers. As the apostle Paul prayed in Romans 15:5–6, "May the God who gives endurance and encouragement give you a spirit of unity among yourselves as you follow Christ Jesus, so that with one heart and mouth you may glorify the God and Father of our Lord Jesus Christ."

> You can survive on your own.
> You can grow strong on your own.
> You can even prevail on your own.
> But you cannot become human on your own.
> FREDERICK BUECHNER

Our bonds of friendship can glorify God, especially when they go beyond simply mutual experiences. The band of brothers extends to fathers who have known the challenges of raising children, with or without disabilities, as is the case with my very dear friend Jeff McNair. Jeff has been one of my family's greatest supports in our journey with Caleb. Not only have Jeff and his wonderful wife, Kathi, given of themselves to spend time with Caleb when Melissa and I needed a break, Jeff has also come alongside me as an advocate for Caleb.

One of the many roles of fathers is to advocate for our children. If your child is school age, you are undoubtedly familiar with the Individualized Educational Plan (IEP) process. At least you should be so that you don't put all the pressure of it on your wife. As grateful as I am for the special-education system in this country, parents need to play an active role in making sure that those with titles in the list of "experts" are not making decisions for our children in a vacuum. We need to be speaking into this process.

On one occasion Melissa and I were having a very difficult time with the IEP team. Despite how obvious it was to us that our non-verbal son needed an improved communication system, the IEP team was resistant to making an investment in new software or staff training. Jeff, who happens to also be a professor of special education, attended our IEP meeting with us, intervening on behalf of Caleb and ourselves. Now let me clarify just how much of a time commitment this took on Jeff's part. This IEP meeting was spread out over three weeks and totaled over twenty-four hours of meeting time. That is a lot of clearing of schedules and sacrifices on Jeff's part, but he was there every step of the way. In the end Caleb received the communication system, and the staff received the training they needed to implement it.

Forming a Beachhead

There are all kinds of brotherhoods: sports teammates, golf buddies, tennis partners, bowling threesomes, business colleagues, charity supporters, neighbors, mission teams, accountability groups, etc. But where can fathers of children with disabilities find strength through loyal relationships with other fathers who understand their journey?

If you're new to the world of disabilities, there are men who can mentor you. If you're a veteran at the systems affecting your son or daughter, you can help other men through support groups, online networks, or one-on-one counseling.

David Lyons, an international vice president of The Navigators, learned a lot about the fellowship of suffering after his twelve-year-old son Ian was diagnosed with cancer. David felt the isolation that fathers of children with special needs experience as they watch a loved one in pain. In his book *Don't Waste the Pain*, David shares a letter he received from a friend:

There is a fraternity of suffering people. It's not an official group, and we haven't posed for a photo yet, but we know each other when we meet. Not one of us applied for membership. Suddenly we found ourselves having been inducted into this order.[2]

During his son's struggle with stage-4 alveolar rhabdomyosarcoma, a very rare cancer that kills 98 percent of its victims, David encountered both the receiving side as well as the giving side of 2 Corinthians 1:4–5: "[God] comforts us in all our troubles, so that we can comfort those in any trouble with the comfort we ourselves have received from God. For just as the sufferings of Christ flow over into our lives, so also through Christ our comfort overflows."

After Ian's funeral David couldn't remember a lot of what people said, but he vividly recalls the comfort of a friend's hand on his shoulder and brothers who simply sat next to him in a silent show of support. In reflection he concluded,

I don't know all of God's purposes for allowing pain into your life. But I know one: He intends to comfort you so that you will comfort others. In fact, He intends the comfort you receive from Him to be so abundant that it can't help but overflow into the lives of others. Once you have entered into another person's pain that comfort can take a lot of different practical forms— listening, talking, serving, or just showing up. But before you can comfort others in these ways, we have to get past the biggest obstacle the Devil puts in our way: self-centeredness.[3]

Have you ever noticed how discouragement, apathy, and sin come into our life when we decide we can handle things on our own? No need for input from others—*I am my own man*, we think. The truth is, anything we can handle alone is temporary. God has given us what we need for an abundant life and marriage, and we will not find it outside of time in Scripture, prayer, and fellowship. There is just no substitute. When we hide God's Word in our heart as Scripture tells us to, we are less likely to sin against God and others.[4] When we come before God in prayer, he meets us at our point of need and gives us strength to meet the challenges at hand.[5] When we stay connected and accountable to brothers in Christ, then we find courage to walk out the Christian faith and be the men we desire to be.[6]

Building Bridges of Support

A man that has friends must show himself friendly.
PROVERBS 18:24, *AKJV*

Have you ever visited the Golden Gate Bridge in San Francisco? It is truly an amazing sight to behold! This engineering marvel boasts two main cables that span the bridge's 7,650 feet. There are 27,572 wires in each of those cables, with a total length that could stretch for 80,000 miles—more than three trips around the earth. The weight of the main cables is 24,500 tons, which allows the bridge to carry a suspension weight of 49 million pounds—all hanging on two cables. And it has withstood numerous major earthquakes!

It reminds me of an Old Testament principle in Ecclesiastes 4:9-10 that still stands as a powerful truth: "Two are better than one, because they have a good return for their work: If one falls down, his friend can help him up. But pity the man who falls and has no one to help him up!"

If you're part of a vibrant church community, you know the value of the greater family of God. All churches should be welcoming and empowering places where parents of children with special needs find friends and advocates ready to walk the difficult road ahead. Sadly, this is not always the case. Many families have found repeated rejection or simply no outreach at all from the churches they've attended. As one man told me, "I hate to sound negative, but except in rare cases, a man stands alone with his special-needs situation. I'm grateful for those rare cases that inspire something different than what now exists, even in the church."

From the beginning God created the body of Christ to build walls against people's discouragement and depression. Christian men can become true brothers who work together in their journey to maturity by embracing life in a community of faith. When churches succeed, fathers of children with disabilities do not face life events alone. They are blessed to receive courage from the trustworthy example of others.

Every time I get a chance to speak to special-needs fathers, I stress the importance of connecting with other dads. While we like to think of ourselves as self-sufficient islands, I have yet to see a father who regretted spending time with other dads. I've attended two different support groups and seen fathers begin to open up and share their challenges, fears, and anxieties. In each case a number of dads in the group shared the same concerns. I shrink to use the term "support group," because we tend to shy away from those things. However, truth be told, we all need support.

I recently received a message from a staff member at Joni and Friends who oversees one of our Family Retreats around the country. She indicated that a new family had just canceled their plans to attend a week at Family Retreat. According to the father of this family, their home had become "toxic." He told the staff member that there was no reason for his family to go to the retreat, because his marriage was over, and he and his wife would soon be getting a divorce.

Clearly, this man needed a friend. I reached out and called him to introduce myself. I told him about my role at Joni and Friends, but I assured him that I was not calling as vice president of the ministry. I wanted to talk as a father and husband. His response was somewhat indifferent as he spoke causally about where his marriage was headed. After offering counsel and encouragement, I asked him to reconsider taking his family to Family Retreat. I suggested that it might help him to be around other fathers (and his wife to be around mothers) who understand their desperate need for healing and restoration. As we ended the call, his last words to me were, "I just don't know. I don't think going will help at all."

To my surprise the family showed up the next day at retreat. They enjoyed the week, especially their interaction with other families. They felt less alone in their struggles. Only eternity will reveal all that God did in this family's life that week, but I know the father left a changed man. Due to his time with other fathers and husbands, he committed to work on the issues in his home and marriage.

Sometimes it doesn't take much for us to become brothers in Christ to one another. A phone call, a visit, or simply letting a father know we're available can make a world of difference to a lonely person. Are you a father who can reach out to another dad? Can you let a man know that you care about his family? Or maybe you are the man who needs to ask for help from another dad. Either way, you are not alone. Reach out.

Paying It Forward

Dave Deuel, whom you met in chapter 1, became part of a family group shortly after his daughter was born with Down syndrome. The seed to do so was planted in him by a doctor, who advised Dave and his wife to take Joanna home and treat her like their other kids. Then he told Dave about another couple that had given birth to a child with Downs the same day Joanna was born and urged him to call this couple for mutual encouragement. Dave says,

> In one short but life-changing conversation, a wise and caring doctor had moved me from personal tragedy to personal mission. We couldn't wait to call the other couple, Jeff and Shirley. My wife and Shirley became close friends almost instantly. Jeff and I were stamped from the same mold—had no siblings, grew up in small towns, and came from solid Christian homes. The compatibility seemed like a breath of fresh air. We were not alone. As we walked into their home for the first time, we were warmly welcomed. We started off by doting over our two little round-faced sweethearts, side-by-side in their carriers. The afternoon passed quickly with chicken on the grill, lots of laughing with a little crying, and plenty of advice exchanged. Toward the end of our time together, someone said, "Hey, we need to form a group for families with children with Down syndrome." Encouraged and blessed, I thought to myself, *we already are a family group.*[7]

God works through Family Groups like Dave's to strengthen homes and open doors for male friendships that might otherwise be missed. It doesn't take much to get started. Just invite another father of a child with disabilities to lunch or ask him and his family over for dinner. You might be surprised how God can go before you to bridge the gap and to build new bonds of friendship.

The Washington State Fathers Network was created to help men pay it forward by sharing whatever life stage they are in with other fathers. Their mission is to promote fathers as crucially important people in their children's and family's lives. Shell says, "We firmly believe men are superb resources for each other and fathers have special needs of their own when it comes to raising a child with a chronic illness or developmental disability."[8]

Benefits of Father's Groups[9]

Anxiety decreased 97%
Feeling of joy increased 67%
Family relationships improved 77%
Having someone to talk to increased 80%
Feelings of helplessness decreased 57%

Dietrich Bonhoeffer, pastor, theologian, and WWII prisoner, loved his brothers and sisters in Christ. His love for them transcended affinity. He wrote in *Life Together*, "The Christian, however, must bear the burden of the brother. He must suffer and endure the brother. It is only when he is a burden that another person is really a brother and not merely an object to be manipulated."[10]

Like those Navy Seals who have committed their lives to one another, we have the privilege and responsibility to band together with other fathers. After all, just as those Seals need to know they can depend on other men who have their backs, we need to know that we have brothers backing us up on this journey called fatherhood.

GROWTH STEPS

1. God has given us what we need for an abundant life of fellowship and prayer.

What are you receiving from being part of the family of God? What are you giving?

2. *Jehovah Shammah*—the Lord Is There. With or without a brother in Christ, you are never alone. The Lord is your companion.

Do you need a fresh awareness of God's presence today? Identify the situation and ask for Jehovah Shammah *to show himself to you.*

3. Read Psalm 46.

Ask God to show you a brother in Christ who needs your encouragement and support right now.

Praise God for Jesus Christ who is your best friend. Thank him for Christian friends who have stood by you and your family in times of need.

CHAPTER 9

Courage to Lead in the Marketplace

BY DOUG MAZZA

Courage is going from failure to failure without losing enthusiasm.
WINSTON CHURCHILL

Sometimes I think I'm one of the few presidents of a corporation or organization who hasn't written a book on leadership. When people have suggested doing so to me, an array of great titles come to my mind that already cover the topic from top to bottom. Bookstore shelves are lined with books on how to manage and motivate employees. The idea that I have something fresh to say in this chapter is therefore a breakthrough for me. My message on leadership springs from decades of trial and error, successes and failures, as well as from observing some mentors of uncompromising faith. Now, as I'm much closer to the end of my career than the start, I believe that I've reached some worthy conclusions.

As men, we tend to derive much of our identity from our careers. When two men meet for the first time, one usually asks, "What do you do?" In earlier chapters we touched on the fact that men are "doers"—it's part of our nature. If there's a problem, we like to solve it. Fathers often believe they need to have all the answers. Just ask us, and we'll probably be happy to tell you! These are not necessarily bad qualities but often do not serve us well as leaders, especially when a problem is unfixable. Honestly, the path of least resistance would be for us to spend long hours finding resolutions for work-related issues rather than face "unfixable" health problems we see when we look, with heavy hearts, into the eyes of our precious children.

Regardless of how significant a role you play at work, your position as the leader of your family must be your highest priority. Being your child's father is the one job only you can do. In spite of how wise or talented you might be, the truth is that your employer can replace you. Your family cannot. And in a family touched by disability, your God-given role as a leader becomes even more critical.

So how do you balance life at work with life at home?

Does one always have to win out over the other?

Is it even possible to succeed at both?

> The truth is that your employer can replace you. Your family cannot.

Redefining Success

The Bible places a high value on work. Proverbs 14:23 says, "All hard work brings a profit, but mere talk leads only to poverty." Work is an essential part of life, and it should be a priority for each one of us. We ought to be diligent in becoming skilled at whatever we choose to do, because our success in the marketplace can bring glory to God. As the senior American executive for more than one automobile company and president of a well-known organization, I'm often asked how I achieved such success. This question always makes me a little uncomfortable, because I don't believe that it's simply my personal achievement. I learned a long time ago that any success I've experienced has been the result of surrounding myself with smart, trustworthy people who encourage me and give me their input. It's like some guy said on the television show *Shark Tank* after convincing two multi-millionaires to invest in his business idea: "It's the law of proximity. Surround yourself with four losers, and you will be the fifth. Surround yourself with one winner, and the sky's the limit!"

The wealthy industrialist and philanthropist Andrew Carnegie understood the power of surrounding himself with high achievers. When a reporter asked Carnegie what he attributed his success to, he responded,

> Well, if you want to know how I got my money, I will refer you to these men here on my staff; they got it for me. We have here in this business a mastermind. It is not my mind, and it is not the mind of any other man on my staff, but the sum total of all these minds that I have gathered around me that constitute a mastermind in the steel business.[1]

Now I'm not suggesting that we run our businesses (or families) like steel barons, but when the "mastermind concept" is embraced by those who recognize that they are operating under divine authority—a God who is ultimately in charge—it's highly effective. As Christians, we find this idea expressed throughout Scripture. In Matthew Jesus assures us that he is there when we gather together in focused prayer,[2] the book of Proverbs talks about how iron sharpens iron,[3] and King Solomon reminds his son that a cord of three strands is not easily broken.[4] Working together with God as the third strand, the Lord promises to direct our paths as we yield to him. In the workplace, this kind of Christ-centered mastermind idea helps everyone own the success of the program and understand how they fit into the big picture, all for the sake of honoring Christ.

At Joni and Friends we've established an integrated leadership culture that breaks down barriers between departments and exposes a project's success as genuinely belonging to the full ministry. For example, our JAF Wheels for the World's international distribution of wheelchairs begins with the prisoners who refurbish the donated wheelchairs. Then the process depends not only upon the cooperation of our field staff, development department, and Christian Institute staff but also on the volunteers at JAF Family Retreats. The success of any JAF ministry program depends on the cross-pollinated success of all other departments. It relies on strong ministry-wide relationships led by strong, godly leaders with a master plan. And when it works, the productivity as well as the stewardship is enormous.

This same biblical concept of striving to work with one mind and one voice is also expressed in Romans 15:4–7:

> For everything that was written in the past was written to teach us, so that through endurance and the encouragement of the Scriptures we might have hope. May the God who gives endurance and encouragement give you a spirit of unity among yourselves as you follow Christ Jesus, so that with one heart and mouth you may glorify the God and Father of our Lord Jesus Christ. Accept one another, then, just as Christ accepted you, in order to bring praise to God.

Integrating Your Leadership Roles

By now you might be wondering what all this talk about integration and leadership has to do with men whose lives are affected by disabilities. For me, it has been the difference between a life of uncertainty and a life of purpose. Whether we're married men, single fathers, or foster fathers, we are the head of our household.

This is a God-given and God-honoring role. Before disability came into our life, many of us were probably looked up to as leaders who managed needs, ideas, and responsibilities—in short, as chief integrators. People turned to us for the plan. Fathers are adept at wearing many hats! In addition to our job title, we may also have been volunteer coaches, teachers, mentors, bill-payers, auto experts, or chief grill masters.

Then our child was born with special needs, and those roles that once demanded our time and attention may have fallen to the wayside or at least become more complicated. When disability enters the picture, we quickly learn that life will never look the same. Teams of doctors, special educators, and therapists start determining the family schedule in ways that begin to infringe on your career goals. The demands of caring for children with special needs have left some men with no choice but to quit their jobs to become stay-at-home dads, a prospect they could not have previously fathomed.

In chapter 3 Dr. Ware shared his courage to face the possibility of giving up a ministry that he loved to care for the son he loved much more. He said, "God knew Matt before we did and would continue to provide for him now. My responsibility was to continue to be a living sacrifice, even if that meant leaving a ministry that I enjoyed in order to work two or three jobs to meet Matt's medical needs!" In time the Ware family's financial needs were met through an unlikely source, so Dr. Ware was able to continue in the ministry.

Earle Rice, on the other hand, is a father who decided to put his career on hold so that his son, Nick, could complete his education. Nick and his twin brother, Kendall, were delivered by an emergency C-section due to a twin-to-twin transfusion syndrome in which Kendall was taking all the vital nutrients from his brother. Although Nick was born with cerebral palsy, he grew to become a gregarious boy and later a confident young man. One day Nick announced that he dreamed of a career in radio broadcasting. Earle was listening and praying:

> As Nick's high school graduation drew near my wife, Betty, and I discussed how we wanted more for our son than what was available in our small hometown. I became more and more nervous about Nick's approaching senior IEP meeting because we knew we needed to discuss a plan for his future. We found a good radio broadcasting program in a small town about 100 miles away. Trusting God all the way, we decided to commit the next two years to helping Nick pursue his passion for radio. Unlike typical parents, we all packed up and moved to college. After college, Nick applied and was accepted into a 9-week radio internship at Joni and Friends. So once again, Nick, Betty and I made a temporary move to California.
>
> As the internship was coming to an end, I started to pray about what was next for Nick and for us. We didn't have a definite plan for Nick and wondered how the Lord would direct. That's when Joni Eareckson Tada invited us to lunch and suggested that we look into the program at Barnabas Prep School in Missouri. Their program goal was for young adults with special needs to develop more independence.
>
> We were reticent at first, but after a visit from a campus representative, we agreed that it was time for Nick to try his wings and live apart from us. In a school environment, he could develop more independence, but still receive the assistance he needed.

Parents like Earle and Betty are willing not only to go the second mile for their children but also to find the courage to let go when God opens new doors.

When my son Ryan was born, I fought tooth and nail to hold onto control of everything but failed miserably. I even thought it was somehow my responsibility to save Ryan. In chapter 4 I detailed how my initial white-knuckled grip turned to surrender. When I accepted my God-given job as Ryan's father instead of his savior, I began to pray earnestly for discernment and wisdom to know what to do in each situation our family faced.

I hate to break this news to you, my friend, but you're not qualified to be in charge—at work or at home. Contrary to what the world tells you—you weren't built for it, and neither am I. We need the One with much greater power at the helm to do the integrating for us. We may not always understand what God is doing, and we don't have to agree with him. We can question or even get angry at God, because he has broad shoulders! He will gracefully handle our complaints. What is nonnegotiable is the fact that he is God! And I'm not—and you're not! What a relief!

This truth is foundational to transforming our leadership at home or in the workplace. Even Jesus, who *is* God, modeled this for us when he was here on Earth. As Philippians 2:5–7 tells us, "Your attitude should be the same as that of Christ Jesus: Who, being in very nature God, did not consider equality with God something to be grasped, but made himself nothing, taking the very nature of a servant." Jesus, our ultimate role model, especially in leadership, went to great lengths to show us that a good leader is a servant leader with his eyes fixed on God. So where do we find the kind of courage we need to be the leader God wants us to be?

Finding Another Kind of Courage

Courage cannot be mandated, but it can be developed. It begins with the four C's:

> 1. *Christ.* Trust that Christ is who he says he is. I can't assume that because you're reading this book, you have a personal, life-altering relationship with Jesus Christ that

guarantees your eternal salvation. If you don't, it's time for you to give serious consideration to accepting God's gift. Or perhaps you need to recommit your life to a relationship you've neglected with the Savior who gave *his* life for *you*. Christ's suffering was more than you and I could possibly bear, and then he miraculously rose from the dead. What more can we ask of God? I invite you to pray right now and make the best leadership decision of your life. Share your new commitment with a pastor or Christian friend. Salvation isn't a secret, it's a celebration!

> *God, I confess that I've been trying to live my life by my rules. My self-reliance is a sin because it ignores what Christ did for me on the cross. Forgive me now as I present myself to you without reservation. Be Lord of my hopes and plans—my family, my career, and my future. Thank you for loving me enough to give me the gift of salvation. Amen.*

2. *Contentment.* Once you dedicate yourself to Jesus Christ, life changes—not because of anything you do, but because of what Christ does! You will begin to redefine "contentment" much as Paul did in his prison cell, where he penned these words: "I have learned the secret of being content in any and every situation, whether well fed or hungry, whether living in plenty or in want. I can do everything through him who gives me strength" (Philippians 4:12–13).

Such contentment is far beyond our earthly goal of being happy. Happiness is an event, but contentment in Christ is a destination! As the father of a child with special needs, do you have contentment? God intends it for you in your current and future circumstances. Contentment requires faith in the love that Christ has for you. It can't be found by running from your troubles, which is tantamount to running from God. *Contentment is laying your head on the pillow at night and knowing that you are right where God wants you to be—regardless of your weaknesses.* That's the spot where God's power shows up best.

Consider God's promise in 2 Corinthians 12:9: "My grace is sufficient for you, for my power is made perfect in weakness." Did you get that? The power of God shows up best in the faithfulness of the weak. Therefore, the more we rely on our own strength, the less we receive the power of God. Sounds like "no contest" to me! Want to be your family's "Superman"? Well then, make your relationship with Christ your phone booth!

3. *Confidence.* Contentment brings confidence! Notice that I said nothing about *liking* your circumstances. Rarely does confidence associate itself with special needs. And having a child with disabilities was probably not on your bucket list. Yet consider the assets that can build your confidence. You have a relationship with Christ, an eternal home in heaven, and you know you're where God wants you. The God of the universe has stepped in and is at your side; he will never leave you nor forsake you. These truths produce tremendous confidence.

4. *Courage.* Paul was a courageous leader. Period! One stoning, and frankly, I'd be done! Yet after Paul was taken to the edge of town, stoned, and left for dead, he got up, dusted off his battered, bloody body and said something like, "Well, that went pretty well!" How do we know that? Because Paul walked to the next town and started preaching all over again. Sounds like Paul had those four C's down.

So take heart! "Stand firm in the faith; be men of courage; be strong. Do everything in love" (1 Corinthians 16:13–14). Join me as a fellow father of a child with special needs. Trust Paul's Jesus—or better yet, trust your Jesus.

The four C's can help you find a level of courage that you couldn't have imagined. Yes, Jesus is *that* good!

Lead with a Servant's Heart: Romans 8:28 Moments

Jesus Christ's example of leadership requires humility and the attitude of a servant. Being called a servant has negative connotations. Who wouldn't prefer being called VP, CEO, The Cake Boss or any kind of boss? The crowds in Jerusalem tried to call Jesus king, but he knew who he was and why he had come. Godly servant leaders who find their identity in Christ can create an environment in which people want to follow not only them but Jesus as well. Their actions demonstrate that their highest priorities are to love and serve Christ. As Colossians 3:23 instructs, "Whatever you do, work at it with all your heart, as working for the Lord."

In order to lead as Jesus did—surrendered to the Father—you don't have to put a Bible on every desk in your company or wear a cross lapel pin. You start by privately inviting Christ into your meetings and decisions through prayer—every meeting, every decision. It may seem unnatural at first, but practice makes, well, almost perfect! Try this and see if, over time, your actions, following a heartfelt prayer before a meeting, aren't more successful. My experience is that inviting God in has a marked effect on outcomes. If you won't invite Jesus Christ in, don't expect him to elbow his way into your life. As Matthew 7:7 says, "Knock and the door will be opened to you." No knocking, no open door. Jesus isn't randomly throwing the door open in your life to see if you're out there somewhere. He has unlimited and eternal patience. He's waiting for your knock.

When we lead families affected by disability, it is easy to reach our human limitations due to pressures and complications. What a relief it is when we trust God to step in and take control! The issues we struggle with may be obvious at home, but our colleagues are often unaware of our additional stress. And as men, we're reluctant to remind our coworkers and employers of it, because we think that our child's disability might make us look weak. In my experience, nothing could be further from the truth.

I actually received one of my most significant job promotions thanks to my son's disability! I can still recall the international CEO telling me why he selected me over the other top contender. We were on an airplane together traveling across the country when our conversation turned to our families. He knew about Ryan's severe disabilities and asked how he was doing. As I finished giving him a quick update, he looked at me and said, "Doug, I had two very good candidates for this new position. I was having difficulty deciding which of the two of you I should hire. But when I understood fully what you have been through with your son and the way you've been able to manage through all that, I realized that this is a man who understands adversity and manages it well. I don't know how you have been able to do that—it must have been very difficult—but I believe that you have a peace and stability about you because of your experience with your son, and that will serve you well as a leader."

This man was not a Christian—he didn't know Jesus—but he saw God's peace in me. In the middle of all the stress and difficulty surrounding my son's disabilities, I would never have imagined that God would use it to place me in such a high position of leadership. Far from sensing weakness, that CEO saw strength—God-given strength. The promotion was one of the first "Romans 8:28

moments" in my life in which all things worked together for good. However, even this pales in comparison to God's ultimate plan for my life. All my business experience has been a training ground for my current work as president of Joni and Friends, where I have the privilege of helping lead an incredible ministry.

Now don't get the wrong idea. No one gets a promotion at work by running around as though his or her hair were on fire and being frazzled in the office because of a disability at home. That's not a step toward corporate success. Neither is being the company stoic. Balance is essential. I do not know how any father of a family affected by disabilities achieves real balance without faith in God. Trust me on this; I have tried it in my own strength. Remember that Someone stronger, more reliable, and ever present is the best platform for balance.

There are two keys to balancing the demands of disability while at work. One key is to embrace our human tendency to compartmentalize the different areas of our lives. This will serve us well as we learn to focus on giving our jobs the attention they demand. This doesn't mean that we should try to hide our family situation, however, because that may serve to further complicate things.

The second key is to embrace our reality by becoming transparent and allowing our children's disabilities to become a part of who we are—that is, the new normal. Life in the business world is hard enough. God will use every situation to strengthen and equip us in ways we can't even imagine from where we stand right now. It is a high calling to bring the lessons of adversity into the marketplace. You must lean into the promise of Romans 8:28: "And we know that in all things God works for the good of those who love him, who have been called according to his purpose." Even if your boss doesn't reward you—even if you don't get that promotion—God is causing things to work together for your good and you are storing up extraordinary treasure in heaven.

God is looking for leaders who have been tested by the fire and have learned to trust him. The challenges are real—more difficult than climbing up the corporate ladder. One president I worked for told me that there was "no room for God in this company" and directed me to stop a lunchtime Bible study. There were countless times when my faith was challenged in the workplace. But that just served God's greater purpose. As I stood firm, people saw how important Christ was in my life. That's when God began to call me to higher levels of responsibility and ultimately into full-time ministry.

I'm not saying that my experience is typical nor that all roads will (or should) lead to full-time ministry. Although God does seem to be calling some wonderful pastors these days, I believe that our country needs more dedicated, principled, and Bible-believing Christian leaders in business. Would our country have been more or less likely to suffer a devastating housing bubble if bank presidents were leading regular Bible devotions, seeking to lead like Jesus, and praying for wisdom in stewardship? This is not a trick question: the answer, obviously, is, "Less likely." Clearly, many good men and women are called by God to lead like Jesus in the marketplace. They are servants who are surrendered to and work under the authority of our heavenly Father. Look for these leaders in your area. It's only lonely at the top if we *choose* to be alone. God will never leave us nor forsake us.[5]

God in Hindsight

The irony of my journey is not lost on me. Thinking back on my experience, I see God directing each step. He revealed the purpose for my life by giving me a son whom I thought had no purpose. The day after Ryan was born, after being up all night, I came home alone and collapsed on the steps of my house. I had hit a wall, and there was nothing left. As the tears streaked my cheeks, I wasn't even thinking about who might be witnessing my breakdown. I was convinced that my son was going to be dead in a few days and that his birth had been a complete tragedy. Now, many years later, I find myself celebrating Ryan's life all over the world, and it never ceases to amaze me! Ryan is my ministry partner. My son revealed the purpose for my life. I owe him everything. He went from being a tragedy in my mind to someone I cannot repay. Is he made in the image of God? You bet. That twisted skull, those bulging eyes, the dislocated jaw— this is the image of God in my life. Ryan is my God-given signpost for what I am supposed to do with my life.

You may be just starting out on this journey and completely unable to see how anything good can come from your child's disability. I am not making light of your daily struggles, nor am I saying, "Snap out of it! Get over it!" What I want you to know is that there are other men who understand your struggles. Although it sounds trite, God promises that he will not give you more than you can handle. But you must endure what he brings you. God has a beginning, middle, and an end to your anguish, and he will show you a purpose for it. The only people who don't get to see God's purposes are those who give up mid-stream. I love this quote from A.W. Tozer: "It is doubtful whether God can bless a man greatly until he has hurt him deeply." Take a moment now to tell God that you are committed to staying the course; you're willing to follow his plan. Also consider sharing this commitment with a brother in Christ who will be faithful to pray for you and your family.

As my coauthor Steve Bundy shares from his own experience, God knows what he's doing with our life, even when it's not always clear to us. When Steve returned from the mission field as a young man, God gave him a job as the head of a long-term-care facility. It was an improbable position for Steve because he didn't have any experience in the healthcare field. He spent his days caring for people with disabilities and learned a lot. Years later his son was born with multiple disabilities. Steve had had no idea that disability was in his future, but God knew and had lovingly prepared him. Eventually Steve became a vice president here at Joni and Friends, where he uses the preparation that God gave him many years before. Though Steve didn't understand it at the time, God was training him for the position of leader in his home as well as in his workplace.

A Leader in Word and Deed

There's one more area of leadership that may not have yet crossed your radar: God needs Christian fathers who will speak up for those who cannot speak for themselves.[6] Our children need advocates. Christian advocacy and service are part of our witness for Christ. God calls us not only to proclaim the gospel but also to demonstrate his love through our actions. Psalm 10:17–18 says, "You hear, O LORD, the desire of the afflicted: you encourage them, and you listen to their cry, defending the fatherless and the oppressed."

Joni Eareckson Tada is one of the most influential disability advocates in our generation. She inspires thousands of men and women to redirect their painful experiences into creative participation in worldwide disability ministries and organizations. Joni says,

> Our wonderful God is doing everything from his end to right what is wrong. But he requires us to partner with him to rescue the fragile, stop abortions, console the dying, minister to orphans, comfort the despairing, heal marriages, halt addictions and bind up the wounds of the brokenhearted. We can be a friend who speaks up on behalf of those who are too weak, too small or too old to speak for themselves.[7]

Here are some ideas to help you learn more about disability initiatives and how to share your views with others:

- Visit websites to understand policies or laws that encroach on the welfare of children receiving special education as well as people with disabilities and the elderly such as Child Advocates, based in Houston, Texas (www.childad vocates.org), or the National Disability Rights Network (www.ndrn.org).
- Join national groups and associations to raise awareness and funding for a disability that affects your family member or friend, such as Autism Speaks (www.autismspeaks. org) or the National Down Syndrome Congress (http://ndsccenter.org/resources/general-information/).
- Contact editors and TV producers who present slanted or inaccurate views about disability research, and share your concerns.
- Create a "watch dog" task force to expose government bills and initiatives seeking to cut funding for disability programs and research.
- Coordinate local letter-writing campaigns that include people with disabilities and the elderly. Personal letters sent to district offices of state or U.S. representatives work best.
- Write opinion pieces and letters to newspaper editors in your state capitol and in Washington, D.C.

Joe Butler, whose son Micah has been diagnosed with both autism and cerebral palsy, admits, "I never really noticed people with disabilities until my son was born." Once Joe's eyes were opened, he had a newfound level of awareness and found his calling. In 2010 Joe and his wife, Jen, founded a non-profit ministry, Ability Tree, Inc. The ministry promotes the need to recognize our children's *a*bilities, not just their *dis*abilities. They also help families by offering trained respite and afterschool care. Joe and Jen know firsthand the exhaustion of parenting a child with a disability, including the myriad appointments with therapists and doctors. Joe, an ordained minister and missionary, observed how few people reached out to help families like his—even in the church.

Joe credits his faith in Christ with strengthening him to face the challenges, and he recently completed a master's degree in disability ministry. He says that too many fathers of children with special needs are carrying a burden they were never meant to carry. "The greatest source of rest is found in God," Joe says. "The Word of God says, 'Come to me, all of you who are weary and carry heavy burdens, and I will give you rest'" (Matthew 11:28, *NLT*).

> When we endure and lay our burdens at the foot of the cross, God can mold us and shape us for leadership—wherever he chooses to place us.

Don't misunderstand—disability is not a Damascus-road experience. It doesn't instantly transform us into spiritual giants. It is a process. We've outlined that it requires trust, faith, and surrender. As our faith grows, the process is accelerated. If our faith shrinks, the process is slowed. When we endure and lay our burdens at the foot of the cross, God can mold us and shape us for leadership—wherever he chooses to place us. God has a plan for you, my friend. You have a purpose. The suffering you face right now is a part of it. Don't run from it. Lean in, and know that the good will come.

Our mastermind is *Jehovah Jireh*. Jehovah Jireh, *God My Provider. With tender-hearted care, you teach me and lead me. Oh, may I never wander! Here's my heart! Take and seal it for thy courts above!*

GROWTH STEPS

1. God created you with natural abilities and interests that can lead to meaningful work.

   What has your career or trade taught you about yourself?

2. God understands the challenges that you face being a servant leader both at home and at work.

   What (or who) has been the greatest influence on you in maintaining a sense of balance between the two?

3. Even in tough situations in the marketplace, God promises to work all things out for your good.

   Can you remember a "Romans 8:28 moment" when you were deeply aware of God's presence in a leadership task? If not, ask God to show you himself in the days ahead.

Praise God for Christians who speak out for those who are too weak to speak for themselves. Consider how you might advocate for adults and children with disabilities.

CHAPTER 10

Courage to Trust in God's Eternal Plan

BY DOUG MAZZA

Life must be lived forward, but can only be understood backwards.
SØREN KIERKEGAARD

Rejoice in our confident hope. Be patient in trouble, and keep on praying.
ROMANS 12:12, *NLT*

What do you say to a father who is facing the possible death of a child?

I've walked in that man's shoes with my son Ryan. And I can assure you that I didn't want to hear Scripture or pious platitudes. I wasn't even sure I wanted anyone around me. If you and your child are facing a life-threatening disability or illness, this book may have been divinely placed in your hands. I'm not saying that it has all the answers. In fact, if I were sitting across the table from you, I might choose not to say a word for a very long time, because I've found that sometimes the mere presence of a good friend is more powerful than conversation. When we try to come up with something to say, we may actually do more harm than good.

Standing on the edge of despair can become almost common-place for families with children who are medically fragile. I remember a time when a coworker of mine showed up to live out the verse "weep with those who weep."[1] As Ryan battled to survive in the ICU, I was experiencing one of my lowest points. I didn't even know what I needed, but my friend Buck—a tough Vietnam War door gunner—somehow knew what to do. Without my asking, he showed up at the hospital and sat silently next to me. Eventually, we went in to see Ryan, who had just come out of surgery. He was still in a coma with his head bandaged so completely that only his eyes peeked through. As Buck stood there with me, he became overcome with emotion and started weeping. I can't explain it, but that moment brought me great comfort. I felt the love and understanding of a true friend.

Most people want to steer clear of us when we're in such a tragic situation. They aren't being cold or uncaring; they simply don't know what to say, and avoidance is easier. Some well-meaning visitors try to share a verse or cliché in an effort to cheer us up. I had one friend actually quote Romans 8:28 with the full assurance that God was working all things together for good as my son barely clung to life in the ICU. While I know that the Bible is true and my friend's intentions were good, the sentiment felt almost unkind. It was definitely unappreciated coming right at that moment.

We often return to the story of Job in the Bible because we relate to his grief as a father. You'll remember how his friends who came to visit were seemingly well intentioned. They started out right by showing up to support their friend who had lost almost everything. But then they blew it by opening their mouths. They started preaching to Job and telling him all the reasons he was suffering, but they were so wrong. They truly had no idea what was happening. Job didn't hesitate to speak up and tell them, "If only you could be silent! That's the wisest thing you could do."[2]

We See But a Glimpse

Job was grieving the loss of his children and struggling to comprehend why his world had been turned upside down. There were no easy answers—there never is when a child dies too early. In his book *Trusting God: Even When Life Hurts*, Jerry Bridges writes,

> Adversity is difficult even when we know God is in control of our circumstances. In fact, that knowledge sometimes tends to aggravate the pain. "If God is in control," we ask, "why did He allow this to happen?"[3]

Bridges lost his mother at age fourteen and later watched his wife succumb to cancer. He wrote the book as a result of his own struggle to understand God's divine sovereignty in light of pain and suffering. Bridges goes on to provide an analogy of each man walking along a path with a thick curtain just ahead, limiting his view of what awaits. "None of us can tell what is beyond that curtain; none of us can tell what events a single day or hour may bring into our lives."[4] Through all life's unknowns, Bridges circles back to the issue of leaning into our faith and trusting in God's goodness. No easy task, especially in light of what we might be asked to face.

What's weighing on your mind today? What uncertainty do you need to bring before your heavenly Father? Philippians 4:6–7 is a favorite passage that many of us have memorized: "Do not be anxious about anything, but in everything, by prayer and petition, with thanksgiving, present your requests to God. And the peace of God, which transcends all understanding, will guard your hearts and your minds in Christ Jesus." David Lyons, whom we mentioned in an earlier chapter, learned to pray *big* prayers as his son, Ian, battled cancer:

As a leader, countless times I'd prayed for wisdom from above. Now, as a parent, I needed supernatural wisdom more than ever. My child's life was on the line! James 1:5 fit like a glove. After exhorting us to embrace trials as friends, James went on to say: "But if any of you lacks wisdom, let him ask of God, who gives to all generously and without reproach, and it will be given to him" (*NASB*). I realized that James's promise of wisdom was especially addressed to those of us in pain. So I prayed. Boy, did I pray!. . . Pain pushes us to stop dinking around with small prayers. You don't ask for a pistol when you really need an army. You don't ask for a bicycle when you really need a truck. Extraordinary needs evoke extraordinary prayers.[5]

At the very end, even when you're facing what seems to be the final battle, prayer is still essential. In the following journal entry David expresses the ongoing importance of praying, even when the answers aren't what you desire:

We've been praying crazy faith prayers here. I feel like one of those pilots in a *Star Wars* movie, strapped in for a life-or-death firefight. I engaged in the spiritual battle in earnest Saturday afternoon. At 11 that night Renee texted me from home to say good night, and I replied that it would be awhile before my head would hit the pillow. I was still stoked and going after it in prayer. But soon the Lord impressed on me that he gives to his beloved even in his sleep. So I slept until about 6 a.m., and then resumed my part in this battle, while Ian carries on his.

I prayed fiercely. I prayed as I wanted others to pray for me. I prayed as we had prayed before, when we'd seen God do the miraculous again and again. But I was about to learn that praying is not always about getting the results we hope for. Sometimes God has something even bigger in mind.

While we pray intently for God's healing to come and spare our children, God's answer sometimes is no. We cry out asking for help to understand God's plan, especially regarding our children with intellectual disabilities. How can they come to know Jesus Christ and find eternal life?

Sharing Jesus, Our Everlasting Hope

Even though my son Ryan has never spoken a word in his life, I'm confident that if he were to die today, he would go straight to heaven. Ryan has never recited the "sinner's prayer" and may not even understand the concepts of sin and repentance. But I believe that God's grace covers those with intellectual disabilities who are unable to grasp such abstract ideas. I also know that people with intellectual disabilities often understand much more than they seem to comprehend. My son, who is now thirty-six years old, has never spoken a word to me, and the doctors say he has the intellect of a six-month-old child. Still I have presented the entire gospel to him and asked him to receive Christ into his heart. I knew that as his father it was my responsibility, even though I have no way of knowing how much Ryan truly understood. It brought me great comfort as well. Did I need to take that step? Maybe not, but if I share the gospel with others, why would I not share it with my own son?

A few years ago I was in Haiti doing relief work after the massive 2010 earthquake. A young boy with severe intellectual disabilities named Judé was brought to our wheelchair distribution center to be fitted with a wheelchair. Judé caught my attention because he made a familiar sound, not a word, but a sound that was similar to one Ryan often makes. I walked to him as he was being lifted into a wheelchair by a physical therapist, much against his will. Instinctively, I gently cradled his face in the palm of my hand, and Judé stopped crying. As I stood there for a moment consoling him, the therapist with us said, "Wow, you've got quite a touch!" I replied, "No, I don't think it's me. I think that God allows people like Judé—and my son—to see and hear things that we can't." While this idea isn't necessarily found in Scripture, I've sensed it with people with severe developmental disabilities and it comforts me.

I have often seen people with severe intellectual disabilities experience unexplainable joy or deep contemplative times as though hearing something on a frequency blocked by my connection to a predictable world. I believe that God can speak to and through all of us. Could it be that people with the innocence of a Ryan or Judé hear that voice more clearly without our worldly filters? I admit I don't know. But I am comforted by the nature of God, the peace of God, the love of God, and by his commitment to people with disabilities as he walked the Earth in the person of Jesus Christ. Christ lives and his love and commitment to those with special needs has not changed.

Yes, God loves people with disabilities. I believe that his grace assures both Ryan and Judé a place in heaven. In 2 Samuel 12 we see that King David felt the same way about the child that he lost. In verse 23 he says, "I will go to him, but he will not return to me." King David was confident that he would see his child again someday. I believe that children with severe intellectual disabilities will be welcomed into God's kingdom when they pass away. As fathers, we can share this comfort and help one another face the future.

Letting Go

We all know that parenting is only for a season, whether a child has a disability or not. But parents of children with life-threatening disabilities are not releasing their precious daughter to her betrothed or delivering their son to a university. Many of them live each day with the thought that someday they'll likely stand before their child's casket.

When Ryan was born, his prognosis was so grim. We were told that he would likely not live past the age of three. It was confining! We felt stuck in a day-to-day kind of existence, hesitant to look beyond the next twenty-four hours. As Ryan continued to defy the odds and outlive the doctors' predictions, I began to embrace the fact that only God knew how many days we would enjoy with our son. Psalm 139:16 assures us that every day of our lives has been written before one of them comes to pass. God knows whether Ryan will reach his fortieth birthday. He knows every detail of your child's life too.

Even so, it is gut-wrenchingly difficult to let go, as David Lyons bravely shares in this description of his son's last days:

> Yesterday afternoon Renee and I had a profound time alone with Ian. He was alert and seemed to be "with" us. Tears were flowing as I said something like this:
>
> Ian, I'm sure that somehow in the midst of all this Jesus is making himself known to you in amazing and personal ways. And we want you to know that however he is leading you, we want you to follow him. As far as we can understand his leading, we believe that he intends to heal you. But if he is clearly telling you that he wants you to leave us and go home to be with him, then we want you to do that. I really mean that. Even though in the coming hours and days you'll hear us intensely battling for your healing in prayer, if Jesus himself is calling you home, go for it. Don't worry about disappointing us. That would be very hard for us, but we'd be happy for you. However, if you hear Jesus calling you to fight, then I want you to FIGHT with all you have. I know this has been incredibly hard for you. But if Jesus is telling you to fight, then he will strengthen you. Don't lose heart, son. Just follow Jesus however he leads you. And he will enable you.[6]

Ian answered Jesus' call home the next day. David later sought solace in the book of Job. He found a man—much like himself—agonizing over the death of a child and struggling to comprehend the *why*.

Dr. Larry Waters, associate professor of Bible exposition at Dallas Theological Seminary, writes extensively on the book of Job. He says, "Life is more than a series of absurdities and unexplainable pains that one must simply endure, it is a life linked with the unseen purpose and destiny of God. . . . God does allow suffering, pain and even death, if it best serves his purpose and destiny for his creation."[7]

Best? How could the death of a child ever serve God's purpose?

God's Plan, Not Ours

If someone had asked Tim Kuck that question after the loss of his four-year-old son, he probably couldn't have fathomed an answer. Now in hindsight, Kuck, COO of Regal Boats and co-founder of Nathaniel's Hope, sees the ripple effect from his son's life and death. But this valuable insight came to Tim only after a season of indescribable grief and depression.

> Our son, Nathaniel Timothy Kuck, was born on June 6, 1997 and died November 13, 2001. His short life was never what I dreamed of for my only son. Proverbs 19:21 tells us, "Many are the plans in a man's heart but it is the Lord's purpose that prevails."
>
> We welcomed Nathaniel home from the hospital when he was only 89 days old and weighing four pounds. His nursery looked like an ICU unit, with feeding tubes, IVs, and heart and oxygen monitors. At first we believed that Nathaniel had an unidentified syndrome, since tests at Boston Children's Hospital were inconclusive. Later, his condition was never completely diagnosed and had

similarities to Craniosynostosis, with other complications, which is a disorder where the skull plates prematurely fuse together, prohibiting brain growth. In spite of Nathaniel's seven major surgeries, our lives settled into a routine with my wife Marie serving as an excellent caregiver and super woman. But underneath my calm mask, stress was taking its toll on me.

When Nathaniel was about 3, I found myself in an "emotional funk." My poor attitudes warned of my pending depression. Oddly enough, I had never had much grace for negative, pessimistic people. I wanted to tell them, "Get a life! Get off the couch, stop whining, and do something." But now *I was the whiner*!

By the grace of God and over time, Tim eventually pulled out of his serious depression. He and Marie determined to do everything possible for Nathaniel and to trust God with the impossible. Life returned to normal for a season. Although Tim rarely traveled because of Nathaniel's condition, in the Fall of 2001 he was invited to speak at a mission conference in another state. I'll let him tell the story:

On Saturday, November 10, 2001, Marie drove me to the airport along with our children: Brianna (9), Ashley (7), and Nathaniel, who was 4. At the curb, I opened the sliding door of the van and kissed my son on the head. Our "little man" was sick, but since he'd spent 150 days of his young life in hospitals, it wasn't unusual.

I spoke in churches on Sunday and Monday. When I talked with Marie the first day, Nathaniel had become a little more congested and was getting breathing treatments. The following night Marie told me she expected to spend the night with Nathaniel sitting upright in an easy chair. At 6:00 a.m., the phone rang and Marie was frantic. She and Nathaniel were in an ambulance, and he was not breathing. The paramedics were doing their best to resuscitate him, but to no avail. She feared that our son was dead. *Without our consent, without our permission, our little boy had changed addresses—from earth to heaven.* His body remained, but his spirit had left. Nathaniel died of a cardiac arrest.

Gripped with grief and indescribable pain, I packed my bags and drove 80 miles to the nearest airport. I sat in the terminal emotionally distraught. There must have been 1,000 people near my gate; many were talking on their cells or working on laptops. Others played with their kids, who were excited about going to Disney World. The whole scene was terribly wrong. I wanted to shout from the top of my lungs, "Stop! Don't you know my son is dead?! It's not right for life to continue as normal. The whole world should pause in silent grief over the loss of this beautiful child." Nothing stopped. Yet, *my world* had forever changed.

My father picked me up at the airport and drove me to the hospital where I embraced Marie and my daughters. Marie led me into a room that held the 23-pound body of my son. Nathaniel had always been frail, but beaming with life and a magnetic smile. Now, he was pale and lifeless in a cold empty room. We were asked to identify his body and release him to the funeral home. Still in shock, we signed the necessary documents and said goodbye.

With one foot in front of the other, we stumbled through the details of burying our child. Dates and service plans were scheduled, yet the idea of burying one whom we loved so much was hard to digest. We decided that the funeral would be a celebration of Nathaniel's short life. Even though we were gripped with his absence, we committed to honor the God who took our son without permission or warning. God had appointed his life and knew him by name: *Nathaniel*, which means "treasured gift from God."

On Nathaniel's Celebration Day, 700 people packed the sanctuary. We felt loved and encouraged by our family and friends. Everything about the service honored both God and our son, but the hardest part for us was closing the casket. The pain felt almost unbearable. Even though we knew that Nathaniel's spirit was no longer in that little body, we didn't want to say a final goodbye. While we believed that we would see our son in heaven, it didn't relieve our present pain.

After the funeral, we took our daughters to south Florida to regroup as a family. We had rarely dined in restaurants without Nathaniel becoming irritated, throwing up or dislodging his feeding tube. Now, for the first time in four and a half years, we had a peaceful dinner. But I didn't want that. I missed my son and all of the chaos that came with him. I felt incomplete without him and wanted him back.

As the waves of grief began to subside, Tim and Marie thought back on their family times with a child who had special needs. They realized that from the time Nathaniel was born, people did not know what to do with their family, even people in the church. Families like theirs just did not fit into a mold. No one asked them out to dinner or over to their house. Babysitters were too intimidated to care for their son due to his health. They knew that some Christians wanted to do more but felt as if they were not equipped to help. That is when the Kucks started a ministry called Nathaniel's Hope.[8]

Joni and Friends is honored to have Nathaniel's Hope as one of our affiliates in ministry. They partner with local churches to develop respite programs called Buddy Break. They host an annual party in downtown Orlando to honor families that have kids with special needs. The festival, Make 'm Smile, is saturated with a spirit of joy and is held on Nathaniel's birthday. Marie Kuck says, "We barely knew what we were doing, but we called on our community to help us cheer up children and parents affected by disabilities. About 600 people attended our inaugural event in 2004. By our Tenth Anniversary in 2013, approximately 20,000 people—including 2,000 kids with disabilities—flocked to Lake Eola Park. Make 'm Smile continues to be a celebration of life—a life that may not have been perfect in man's eyes, but was perfect in God's eyes."

Isn't that just like God! A four-year-old boy who never walked, talked, or ate by mouth has shown thousands of people that every life has a God-appointed purpose. Nathaniel's smile continues to shine the light of hope upon hurting families who need to know the love of God.

Estate Planning for Our Children

As difficult as it is to prepare for the potential loss of our children, we must consider the possibility that we might die before they do. One of the most serious worries on any father's heart is the question, "What will happen to my child and my family if I'm no longer here to provide for them?"

Much like wise leaders create succession plans for businesses, a caring father must consider his family's estate planning needs. Often these matters seem too sad to talk about and are set aside with a promise to handle them later. Unfortunately, though, we're not promised ample notice of when we will be called home to be with Jesus. These issues became a real concern for me when I faced a health crisis in November 2012. For the first time I realized that Ryan might outlive me.

Over the years I'd had some serious surgeries, but each time I felt certain that with excellent doctors and good medical care, I'd get back to my old, usual self. This time something was different; I could feel life draining out of me. I remember being in the Intensive Care Unit and watching the clock. A severe blood infection was out of control. Every twelve hours my body would convulse uncontrollably for four continuous hours, causing pain in my joints and sapping what strength I had left. Among the beeping of machinery, the only thing I could see in the functional room was the clock. It was midnight. I knew from experience I had thirty minutes until the next wave of uncontrollable convulsions would sweep over me. My health was spiraling downward—I was so weak that I could barely raise my arms. In that moment, I knew I had no human reserve to survive what was coming. I started to pray. "Lord, you've given me 1 Corinthians 10:13 for strength for almost twenty years. But now, I've endured about all I can endure. I have no more strength of my own. I'll need your strength if I'm going to survive. Father, may I borrow your strength?" When I awoke at 4:00 a.m., I somehow felt strangely comforted. I realized the attack that I feared had not occurred. With the strength I had, I began praising God! I knew I had turned a corner. God still had things for me to do. The "what-ifs" began playing in my head, and I was glad about the fact that I had put a plan in place for Ryan and my family.

There are a few practical steps that all parents should take to protect their children, especially if they have a son or daughter with a disability. Every family should establish a living trust with a selected conservator for the children. Hire an attorney to make it formal and legal. Otherwise, the government will take over and make critical decisions about your child's future—and no one will care as much as you do.

A special-needs trust is a legal document containing instructions directing the management and distribution of the resources placed in the trust. The person creating or funding the trust is the grantor. The person who receives the benefit or on whose behalf the trust was created is the beneficiary. The trust allows you to leave any amount of money to your child without jeopardizing government benefits. Funds in a special-needs trust can make a big difference in quality of life by paying for things such as insurance, personal care attendants, or rehabilitation. A number of good organizations are available to advise families in establishing a special-needs trust such as the Special Needs Alliance[9] and the World Institute on Disability.[10]

Whether choosing a family member or a friend, it is essential to consider a responsible person as your child's conservator. Make sure that he or she will genuinely care about your child when you're absent—don't choose someone who simply feels obligated. A conservator doesn't have to have a lot of money—what they need is a lot of heart. If you don't have someone in mind, begin praying for the Lord to bring the right person into your life.

Once you've selected a conservator, begin including that person in some family activities and specifically in strategic meetings regarding your child, such as his or her school Individual Education Plan (IEP). Invite the conservator along as an observer so that he or she will have a better idea of your child's abilities and reactions. Discuss every aspect of your child's future from finances to health care to living arrangements and the basics of day-to-day life. Don't leave the important things up to chance or interpretation. Tell the conservator what you think and how you feel about your child's future. Involvement is the key to helping him or her understand how you approach decisions, and it will help to create a smooth transition if one becomes necessary.

My son Ryan has a big smile that can light up a room, and he flashes it whenever I show up to visit. It's the greatest thing ever. Though he is blind and has never been able to speak, he has many different sounds that he uses to communicate. You have to get to know Ryan to understand his different sounds. One of his sounds means, "I'm really glad to see you." That's when his smile comes out too. When Ryan hears me call his name, he breaks into that big smile, makes his "I'm glad to see you" sound, and gets very active. It's clear that he's excited that I'm there. He has another sound when he's uncomfortable or in pain. And another when there's a conversation going on and he wants to participate. It's as if he's somehow talking back to us. He becomes especially vocal when we're not talking about him! Somehow he knows when we're talking about him, because he'll sit silently. But when the topic of conversation turns away from him, he'll chime in and make his sound, seemingly saying, "Can we talk about me again?" And finally, he has a sound to let us know that he's done with our visit. He makes it very clear when he's ready for a visit to end.

These are the types of things that can only be learned by spending time with someone. That's why it's so important to involve a future conservator early; that way they can truly get to know your child. Yes, you want to select someone who is competent to handle the legal and financial matters—but you also want that person to genuinely care for your child's best interests. I've visited my son at times and could tell from listening to him that he was in pain. Once I grabbed a nurse and asked her to take a look. She came back and said, "You're right. Ryan has an ear infection." If you don't understand a child's unique ways of communicating, you'll miss important things like that. Find someone who will personally take the time to get to know your child.

No Easy Answers, Just Truth

We started this book with a difficult question from Steve's young son Jaron: "How big is God?" In each chapter we've shared stories of real people who are facing tough circumstances in families affected by disabilities. My prayer is that you have considered that God is big enough to handle whatever it is that you and your child encounter today and in the days ahead. This is true courage, my friend—to get up each day and do the next right thing. To trust God's plan one day—maybe one hour—at a time. Perhaps the best encouragement I can offer comes from what the Lord said to a man named Joshua. With these words, God encouraged Joshua to lead his chosen family, the Israelites:

> Be strong and courageous. Do not be terrified; do not be discouraged, for the LORD your God will be with you wherever you go (Joshua 1:9).

How is it possible for us to do this? Because the God of the universe willingly sacrificed his own son, we can rest in the assurance that he cares about our fears as well as our children's pain and suffering.

In exploring the *why* question in his book *The Question That Never Goes Away*, Philip Yancey writes, "Because of Jesus, we have the assurance that whatever disturbs us, disturbs God more. Whatever grief we feel, God feels more. And whatever we long for, God longs for more."[11] The apostle Paul expressed it best in 1 Thessalonians 4:13–14:

> Brothers, we do not want you to be ignorant about those who fall asleep, or to grieve like the rest of men, who have no hope. We believe that Jesus died and rose again and so we believe that God will bring with Jesus those who have fallen asleep in him.

Take courage, my brother, in God's eternal plan for you and your family, living each day in the hope of our Savior and coming King, Jesus Christ!

GROWTH STEPS

1. Prayer changes things and brings great comfort in the midst of great pain.

   What do you need prayer for right now? Write your prayer needs down and send them to Joni and Friends, where we will pray for your specific requests. Submit prayer requests at http://www.joniandfriends.org/response/.

2. The heart of parenting requires that we learn to let go of our children at various stages of their lives.

   Think about the various stages of your child's life. Consider what the next step might look like and how you can trust God by letting your child go to live out God's divine plan.

3. God *Jehovah*, the Great I AM, the Self-Existent One—never changing. We can never understand him completely—and if we could, he wouldn't be God!

   Read Psalm 102, and use it as your daily prayer.

Another Kind of Courage

STUDY GUIDE

Chapter 1

Courage When There Are No Answers

It is natural for fathers of children with disabilities to wrestle with feelings of depression and isolation. Questions over suffering and trusting God in the midst of it have plagued men since the Fall. Admittedly, it's easy to feel lost at times. Younger fathers may worry that they lack role models to guide them in being a father to a child with disabilities. Some dads may be concerned about how they will provide for their wives and other children, while walking the minefield of special needs. Single fathers are often overwhelmed by trying to be both mom and dad while keeping a full-time job. But God never leaves us alone to work through the maze of medical, social, and emotional issues that we face on a daily basis! God is *bigger* than the nagging confusion we experience. He is ever-present, providing constant companionship as we travel this uncertain path of disability.

Discussion Questions
1. What scares you the most about your child's disabilities? Who or what has helped you deal with your anxieties?
2. God invites you to trust him, recognize his work, and believe that he will answer your prayers and meet your needs. What are the desires of your heart? Proverbs 3:5-6
3. What does 2 Corinthians 12:9-10 tell you about the connection between manhood, strength, and weakness?

Action Steps

- **Head** – My beliefs about God shape how I live. I will examine my faith's impact on my relationship with God and my family.
- **Heart** – When my dreams appear to be crushed under the load of disabilities, I will trust God's righteousness and let him carry my fears.
- **Hands** – I will spend time with like-minded friends to support our mutual beliefs and grow deeper in our faith.

For Group Leaders

Some men don't enjoy talking about themselves and their needs. Open this session with a humorous story about your own father or children. Invite others to chime in with their stories. Assure group members that there is no pressure to discuss their feelings. Strive to create a safe place by encouraging a respect for confidentiality. Acknowledge that fathers may be in different stages of parenting, and their children may have various disabilities ranging from mild to severe. Observe how the men in your group relate to disabilities in different ways and point out common experiences.

For Further Study

- *Why, O God?: Suffering and Disability in the Bible and the Church* by Larry J. Waters and Roy B. Zuck (Eds.). Wheaton, Illinois: Crossway, 2011.

Chapter 2

Courage When Life Spins Out of Control

When life seems to be spinning out of control, it is important to remember that *God* is still in control—no matter how difficult things may be. God is sovereign over the entire universe, and yet he is with you in the midst of *all* of your circumstances. When he looks at you, he sees a child made in his image, whom he deeply loves. Rather than seeing yourself through the lens of feelings of failure, regret, or shame, learn to see yourself as God sees you. Ultimately, it all comes down to perspective: how we view God and how we view ourselves. Cultivating this "God's-eye view" is only accomplished by sharing your fears and worries with the One who made you and deliberately placing him at the center of your world. When your eyes are fixed on him, you are able to face the "chaos" of your life with peace and hope.

Discussion Questions
1. In this chapter, Brent Olstad speaks of learning to engage in "meaningful waiting." How hard is it for you to play the waiting game? What are some of the things you have learned about waiting?
2. In the Garden of Gethsemane, Jesus agonizingly poured out his heart to his Father, surrendering himself to the Father's will for his life. How long has it been since you shared your deepest emotions with God in prayer? Have you truly surrendered your role as the father of a child with disability to your Father?
3. Jesus told us that we would face "trouble" in this life, but he also promised his peace. Is peace becoming an increasing reality in our lives? How does John 14:27 shed light on this truth?

Isaiah 40:31; Matthew 26:36-39; John 16:33

Action Steps
- **Head** – I will find my identity in Christ and trust the gift of peace that he offers me.
- **Heart** – I will intentionally engage my heart and mind in prayer, praise, and worship in the midst of my struggles.
- **Hands** – I will encourage those around me who are struggling. I will work out my own feelings of insecurity, anxiety and anger by finding practical ways to care for those who are sad and need encouragement.

For Group Leaders
Discussion of this chapter's content may spark some raw emotions. It's important to emphasize that God understands our deepest, most heartfelt emotions—even our feelings of anger, despair, and hopelessness. He remains present to us, and offers his comfort and strength, in the midst of those feelings. Being honest with God is the first step to moving forward with him on the journey of faith to which we have been called.

For Further Study
- Joni and Friends TV Episode— "Ryan: A Legacy of Hope" http://www.joniandfriends.org/television/ryan-legacy-hope/

Chapter 3

Courage in the Face of Pain and Suffering

Though pain can be horrendous, it has eternal purpose in God's economy. God permits suffering to draw us closer to himself and deepen our understanding of his sovereign plan. This universal experience has the ability to fill our hearts with love and compassion for a hurting world. As we find courage to surrender our pain to God, we are conformed more and more into the likeness of his Son. Suffering forces us to take our focus off of ourselves and put it on Jesus Christ, who gives us the strength to endure. In the midst of anguish (our own or a loved one's), a hard heart can be softened, and one's character tempered, which brings glory to God. The world doesn't understand this logic.

Divine healing, then, is most importantly *spiritual*—transforming and restoring us to a right relationship with God—rather than *physical*; while the former does not rule out the latter, physical healing is not *necessary* for spiritual healing to occur.

Discussion Questions
1. When the pressure is on, we need a source of strength that will enable us to hold up under its heavy weight. Who or what is your source of strength? Why?
2. Hebrews 12:1-3 charges us to "run with perseverance the race marked out for us" and to "fix our eyes on Jesus, the author and perfecter of our faith." How are these two ideas related?
3. Who is your role model for suffering? What stands out to you about their character?

2 Corinthians 1:8-10; Habakkuk 3:19

Action Steps

- **Head** – I will seek answers to my questions about pain and suffering in God's Word and lean on his promises for my strength.
- **Heart** – I will confess in prayer my obstacle to faith in Jesus Christ. I will pray for others that are enduring seasons of pain and request prayer for my own weakness.
- **Hands** – I will take time to visit a hospital, health care facility, or a home to sit with someone who is suffering. I will seek to be the hands and feet of Jesus to a hurting family.

For Group Leaders

Some men may be struggling with the question of why God doesn't or hasn't "healed" their child. This issue is potentially a significant roadblock to faith and growth in one's relationship with Christ. Allow men to discuss their doubts without judgment; create a safe place. This chapter can help fathers develop a practical "theology of suffering" to understand what suffering is and why we must suffer. These are complex questions that won't be fully satisfied this side of heaven. However, God offers us miraculous peace of heart and mind in the midst of our human condition (John 14:27).

For Further Study

- *A Place of Healing: Wrestling with the Mysteries of Suffering, Pain, and God's Sovereignty* by Joni Eareckson Tada (Colorado Springs, Colorado: David C. Cook, 2010).
- *A Long Obedience in the Same Direction: Discipleship in an Instant Society* by Eugene H. Peterson, 20th Anniversary Edition (Downers Grove, Illinois: IVP Books, 2000).

Chapter 4

Courage to Surrender Control

Your arms are too short to box with God.
ALEX BRADFORD

Surrender is at the core of what it means to follow Christ. Yet this key concept is often misunderstood—it is not equivalent to defeat, and it is not the same thing as quitting. Surrendering to God means relinquishing our own need to be in control, and allowing him to take his rightful place as the one in charge. We must invite God to assume this place of authority in our lives—he won't force his way into the position. It also involves dying to our love of ourselves and our toys, and living for God and others. In exchange for this surrender, Jesus gives us all of himself—his strength, his grace, and his peace—and we are empowered to keep walking on the journey, even in the face of lingering unanswered questions.

Discussion Questions
1. Are there any roadblocks in your life that are keeping you from surrendering control of your life to God?
2. How might an understanding of God's love impact those roadblocks and the power they have over you?
3. Pride and idolatry can be powerful obstacles to yielding control to God. In what ways do these temptations manifest themselves in the context of being a father of a child with a disability? How can these temptations be overcome?

1 John 4:18; James 4:6; Exodus 20:3-4

Action Steps

- **Head** – I will spend time identifying relevant biblical passages that address my roadblocks to faith.
- **Heart** – I will talk to God about my obstacles to surrendering control of my life to him. I will ask a trusted friend to pray with me about overcoming these issues.
- **Hands** – I will write a couple of Bible verses on cards and post them in my car, closet, and desk to remind me of God's power to guide my life and my family's future.

For Group Leaders

This chapter represents a crucial turning point in the focus of this study—from the attempt to *understand* why God has permitted one's child to experience disability, to questions of how to *respond* to the realities of being a father to a child with a disability. Central to this transition is the process of relinquishing control to God—control of one's heart, one's life, and one's family. For some members of your group, this may be a time for them to place their faith in Christ as their Savior—here, your role as an evangelist is vital. For others, there may be obstacles standing in the way of their yielding control to God; chief among these are often idolatry and pride. Here, your role is to try to help men identify the idols that keep them from placing their trust in God. Some fathers may still be struggling with deep-seated fears and anxieties that are keeping them from allowing God to be in charge. As you display the heart of a shepherd you'll help men understand that Jesus is the Great Shepherd, who is able to meet each need.

For Further Study

- *Brokenness: How God Redeems Pain and Suffering* by Lon Solomon. (Potomac, Maryland: Red Door Press, Inc., 2010).

Chapter 5

Courage to Grasp the Servant's Towel

The things you do matter to God.
You matter to God.
And when you serve him,
You are showing that he matters to you.
AUTHOR UNKNOWN

Christian service does not come easily or naturally to most men, because it stretches us beyond our comfort zone. Even the men in Jesus' day must have scratched their heads when he used the words "servant" and "great" in the same sentence. In Bible times "great" men lorded over lowly servants. But Jesus spoke plainly, saying, "Whoever wants to become great among you must be your servant" (Matthew 20:26). By word and example, Jesus taught that service is the gateway to leadership. A true leader cannot accomplish much without having a servant's heart. And when this kind of service is motivated by love, it can leave a legacy that will outlast the leader, and bring glory to God.

S. Truett Cathy, founder of Chick-fil-A, built the nation's second largest quick-service chicken restaurant chain on a philosophy of service. "Nearly every moment of every day we have the opportunity to give something to someone else—our time, our love, our resources," said Truett. "I have always found more joy in giving when I did not expect anything in return."

Discussion Questions

1. In what ways has our culture shaped our thinking about family, fatherhood, service, and greatness?
2. How do you need to transform your thinking in order to be a more effective servant?

3. Love should be the prime motivation for service. How would you rate your love level? Is it unconditional, like Jesus`?

Mark 10:43-45; Romans 12:1-2; 1 Corinthians 13:1-13

Action Steps
- **Head** – With Jesus Christ as my model, I will look for divine interruptions in my day and take time to assist someone in need.
- **Heart** – What are the most significant barriers to your engaging in service? Spend some time praying for one another about these barriers.
- **Hands** – I will find some specific ways to serve my wife and children this week.

For Group Leaders
Some members of your group may be eager for direction with regard to ways in which they can engage in service; it may be helpful to have a prepared list of suggested service ideas that you can share with them—preferably one tailored to the specific context (church, school, etc.) in which you are leading this group. You might also discuss with your members the possibility of organizing a group service project.

For Further Study
- "Interview with Doug Mazza," Joni and Friends Radio broadcast featuring Joni Eareckson Tada and Doug Mazza, 06/18/13, available at http://www.joniandfriends.org/radio/5-minute/interview-doug-mazza/

Chapter 6

Courage to Keep the Marriage Covenant

Have you ever imagined the joyous bliss Adam and Eve must have known in those early days in the Garden of Eden? Talk about a terrific honeymoon! While most couples start out dreaming of paradise, unfortunately, many end up lost in a nightmare. Still, marriage remains a mysterious, God-given blessing that can be life's most deeply satisfying and fulfilling relationship, even when—indeed, often *because*—a child with a disability enters the picture.

The key to a successful marriage is to invite Jesus to be the head of your home. He can be the partner who secures the rope on the uphill climb. He will alert you to the pitfalls of an unhealthy marriage such as breakdowns in communication, anger, and pride. Anger is often rooted in fear of the unknown, which can produce feelings of anxiety and insecurity that are expressed as resentment. You can overcome these destructive tendencies by (1) learning your wife's communication style and intentionally fostering times of genuine communication; (2) relying on the Holy Spirit's power to teach you how to respond to the challenges of marriage and how to parent a child with a disability; and (3) taking time to be alone with God to seek his wisdom and guidance.

Discussion Questions

1. How long has it been since you and your wife had a dream date or spent intimate time discussing your marriage and family? What does she enjoy doing for fun?
2. What light does Christ's relationship with the Church shed on our relationship with our wives? How do Jesus' interactions with his Body, the Church, model ways in which we ought to interact with our spouses?

3. Couples with successful marriages learn to forgive one another and move through the tough times with sacrificial courage. What do you need to forgive? What do you need to sacrifice?

Ephesians 4:31-32; 5:22-33

Action Steps
- **Head** – I will cling to the promises of God and follow the instructions for marriage found in God's Word.
- **Heart** – I will love my wife and spend time praying with her and for her. I will help carry her burdens and encourage her walk with God no matter how difficult the struggle.
- **Hands** – I will honor my marriage vows by preferring my wife above myself. I will work hard to provide for her needs and those of my family.

God is *for* your marriage, and struggling marriages *can* be healed!

For Group Leaders
Some men may be experiencing serious struggles in their marriages. In addition to offering prayer support, encouragement, and practical assistance, you may need to be prepared to refer one or more of them to pastoral or professional counseling services. It is helpful to provide the names and contact information of several Christian counselors in your area as you begin discussing this chapter. Consider inviting a well-qualified, family counselor to meet with your group for a Q & A, as well as a pastor who can pray for couples affected by disabilities.

For Further Study
- Joni and Friends TV Episode #13, Season 1 – "For Better or for Worse," featuring Ken & Joni Tada and Mike & Renee Bondi, http://www.joniandfriends.org/television/better-or-worse/
- *Joni & Ken: An Untold Love Story* by Ken & Joni Eareckson Tada with Larry Libby (Grand Rapids, Michigan: Zondervan, 2013)

Chapter 7

Courage to Raise Godly Siblings

Siblings of children with disabilities long for a father's respect and suport. This will require intentionality on your part since siblings may worry about adding more stress on their parents. They often have the same fears and questions that keep you awake at night. A brother may be anxious about protecting his sibling at school or in social situations. Or a sister may fret about going places with her friends due to the high cost of her brother's care.

As a father, you must invest quality and quantity time in assuring siblings that they're loved unconditionally. Get on their level. Grieve with them when they grieve, and rejoice with them when they are happy.

You play a powerful role in helping your children find their own identity and security in Jesus Christ. With God's grace and your guidance, siblings of children with disabilities can fulfill their unique, God-given roles in life. Ultimately, your task is to guard your family as a shepherd guards his sheep, tending faithfully to *all* the "sheep in your flock" so they feel safe and secure under your care.

Discussion Questions

1. How can you use the adolescent experiences that shaped you to help guide your children?
2. When do you feel closest to your child? How can you facilitate more of these times?
3. How are you modeling the Christian values that you hope to see in your children's lives?
4. What could you do this week to show your children that they are special in your eyes?

Proverbs 22:6, Matthew 6:25-34; Philippians 4:6-7; Colossians 3:12-14, 21

Action Steps
- **Head** – I will read and meditate on God's Word with my children and help them discover their spiritual gifts and talents.
- **Heart** – I will be sensitive to my children's questions, fears, and anxieties, knowing we can pray about them together and trust God with our cares.
- **Hands** – I will plan practical activities to encourage my children on a regular basis.

Deuteronomy 32:45-47; Psalm 8:2; 1 Peter 5:7

For Group Leaders
Some men in your group may not have had the benefit of good father role models or other leaders in their life. Consider who you might be able to point to in your church or local community as examples of good leadership, particularly when it comes to raising godly children.

For Further Study
- Visit Kid's Corner at Joni and Friends at http://www.joniand friends.org/kids-corner/
- Visit a Sibshop in your area or start one at church. http://www. siblingsupport.org/sibshops/index_html
- *Parent's Guide to the Spiritual Growth of Children: Helping Your Child Develop a Personal Faith,* by John Trent, Rick Osborne, and Kurt Bruner (Colorado Springs, Colorado: Focus on the Family, 2000; Tyndale House Publishers rev. ed., 2003).

Chapter 8

Courage to Stand as Brothers

If you are fortunate enough to have one true friend who knows all about you and still likes you, you're uniquely blessed. Raising children is not a job for the "Lone Ranger." In his book *The Father Connection*, Josh McDowell describes fatherhood as "the most frightening, most important, and most rewarding job in the world."[1] No man is smart enough to succeed without the support and encouragement of others. Strong friendships are crucial to navigating a sense of helplessness and isolation that comes too easily to fathers of families affected by disabilities.

A powerful antidote to these barriers is the time you spend in Scripture, prayer, and fellowship. By connecting with other men in genuine community, you can overcome discouragement, apathy, and even sin. Men's support groups glorify God and become a "band of brothers" standing together in crisis. Groups can also focus on service and advocacy for families who are weak. Above all, whether you are giving support or receiving it, you're never alone—so take the risk and reach out.

Discussion Questions

1. Who was your closest friend growing up? What would he have said are your best qualities?
2. Have you been hurt by an unfaithful friend? If so, ask God for strength to forgive and to stay open to new acquaintances.
3. If Jesus called upon his twelve disciples—his friends—to walk with him, why wouldn't you do the same?

Psalm 133; Proverbs 17:17; John 15:13; Hebrews 13:1-2

Action Steps

- **Head** – I will allow the truths of Scripture to challenge aspects of my personality that get in the way of forming authentic friendships. I will step out of my comfort zone to join a faithful group of like-minded men.
- **Heart** – I will renounce my pride and self-sufficiency and look to other fathers for support and accountability. I will pray for my brothers in a spirit of humility and unity.
- **Hands** – I will find ways to use my experiences and talents to serve friends at church and in my community, knowing it will glorify God.

For Group Leaders

In this age of high-speed connectivity, men are slow to connect in "real time." Computers have replaced meaningful friendships with instant updates. Sure, we may know where someone is having lunch or what they're listening to, but we don't know their hearts and minds without connecting with them. Some men aren't sure they need or want to connect with other men, and those who want relationships may not know how to find them. If this is the case, encourage your group to examine Scripture to discover the nature of Christian friendship and how such godly friendships can be developed.

For Further Study

- *The Father Connection* by Josh McDowell (Nashville, TN: B&H Publishing Group, 1996, rev. 2008).
- "We Band of Brothers," Joni and Friends Radio broadcast featuring Joni and Ken Tada, 10/13/13, available at http://www.joniandfriends.org/radio/5-minute/we-band-brothers1/

Chapter 9

Courage to Lead in the Marketplace

Leaders are always the highest-priority targets in any war. . . . Cut off the head and the body dies. The body in this case is your family—you are the head. One way to fight back and be the leaders God created us to be is to be aware of our roles, our responsibilities, and our influence with those we lead.[2]
RICK JOHNSON, *BETTER DADS, STRONGER SONS*

Christian leaders must redefine "success" in terms of its ultimate dependence on God, as well as its interdependence on others. Your goal must be to model for others the strength, peace, and stability that come from surrendering to the Father and engaging in service on behalf of those who are unable to speak for themselves. Such leadership requires balancing the many hats you wear every day, most notably those you wear at home. Integrating your various roles becomes possible only when you let God lead. This frees you to identify with Christ and to serve with your eyes fixed on God.

Discussion Questions
1. How is your success dependent on God? How can God use you to help others be successful?
2. What lessons can be learned from how Christ dealt with adversity? What does it look like to bring these lessons into the workplace?
3. What part does your child's disability play in your work and in your life's purpose? In the context of being the father of a child with a disability, what does it mean to "work with God as the third strand?"

Philippians 2:3-4; Hebrews 4:14-16; Ecclesiastes 4:12

Action Steps
- **Head** – I will find my identity in Christ. I will surrender myself to the Father, as Jesus did. I will spend time in Scripture to get to know *Jehovah-Jireh,* God My Provider.
- **Heart** – I will tell God my greatest fears about leading like Jesus in the marketplace.
- **Hands** – I will practice leading like Jesus in my home by working alongside of my family in every daily task and by helping at church.

For Group Leaders
Leadership is a topic that may bring up past mistakes and failures. Some men may secretly feel that if all their children were typical, they could do a better job at work and at home. They may have not considered how business itself can be a calling. Challenge the group to consider the fact that business can be a highly "spiritual" endeavor in which a man can live out his vocation by exercising his gifts and abilities to serve others at work and at home.

For Further Study
- "When Disability Hits Home," Joni and Friends TV Episode Featuring Chuck Colson and R.C. Sproul http://www.joni andfriends.org/television/when-disability-hits-home/
- *Leading with a Limp: Take Full Advantage of Your Most Powerful Weakness* by Dan B. Allender (Colorado Springs, Colorado: WaterBrook Press, 2008).
- *Lead Like Jesus: Lessons from the Greatest Leadership Role Model of All Time* by Ken Blanchard & Phil Hodges (Nashville, Tennessee: Thomas Nelson, 2005).

Chapter 10

Courage to Trust in God's Eternal Plan

One of the biggest issues parents have with God's plan is that they can't see his purposes ahead of time for their children's lives. Many great eulogies have been written, but their content is delivered in hindsight. As Christians, we are called to carry a vision—a "future-sight"—for those who die before us. It is called *hope*. This hope is so wonderful that it is indescribable: "No mind has conceived what God has prepared for those who love him" (1 Corinthians 2:9).

Yet, hope is not easy to take hold of in a culture where children with disabilities fight for acceptance and become pawns in health care issues. It doesn't seem fair that the precious ones God entrusts to us would be taken away. We don't understand, but we can trust a loving Father who grieved the sufferings of his own Son, Jesus Christ, and who understands our suffocating sadness. God asks us to believe that death is not our final destination. In facing his own mortality, Dr. Billy Graham affirms this: "We are not meant for this world alone. We were meant for Heaven, our final home. Heaven is our destiny, and Heaven is our joyous hope."[3]

Discussion Questions
1. In what way can you see God's hand at work in your child's life? How might this provide hope for your current circumstances?
2. What does it mean to "walk in faith" in the large and small incidents of daily life?
3. Have you shared the Gospel with your children? Pray for the courage to share your faith.
4. According to 2 Corinthians 1:3-5, what is the purpose for your sufferings?

2 Corinthians 5:1; Hebrews 11:1-3; Romans 8:32; Romans 6:23

Action Steps
- **Head** – I will spend time reading biblical passages about hope. I will strive for a mature Christian prayer life to find the courage I need in uncertain times.
- **Heart** – I will share my faith and lead my children to a personal walk with God. I will share the comfort that I've received with others, especially my family members.
- **Hands** – I will consider creating a special needs trust to protect my family. I will put my hope into action by helping hurting and grieving families in my church and community.

For Group Leaders
This chapter emphasizes the need to take practical steps in estate planning for the future of one's family, including appointing a legal conservator for a child with disabilities. Since some men may not have considered this need previously, be prepared for questions with an informative list of resources in this area or with a guest speaker such as a lawyer in your church. For answers to "Frequently Asked Questions" (FAQs) about special needs trusts, visit the FindLaw.com website at http://estate.findlaw.com/trusts/special-needs-trusts-faq-s.html.

For Further Study
- *Nearing Home: Life, Faith, and Finishing Well* by Billy Graham (Nashville, TN: Thomas Nelson, 2011).
- *Don't Waste the Pain: Learning to Grow through Suffering* by David Lyons and Linda Lyons Richardson (Colorado Springs, CO: NavPress, 2010).
- "Holding on to Hope" Joni and Friends TV Episode #11, Season 1 http://www.joniandfriends.org/television/holding-hope/

Another Kind of Courage Contributors

James Achilles has served as a member of the Executive Board of Joni and Friends Sacramento and as an elder and worship leader at Providence Bible Church in Rocklin, California. He has been active with Joni and Friends since 2004. He is a music teacher at Wheatland High School and Bear River Middle School. He has a B.A. in music education and a Master of Divinity in Bible Exposition from The Master's Seminary. Jim and his wife, Deanna, have three grown children.

Pastor Bob Bjerkaas has served as the pastor of Church in the Canyon in Calabasas, California, since 2007. He is currently working toward completing his doctoral degree in ministry from Reformed Theological Seminary. Bob received his M.Div. from Chesapeake Theological Seminary and earned a Th.M. through Reformed Theological Seminary. Bob has been married to his wife, Kerrie, since 1997. They have four children: Christopher, Margaret, Timothy, and Nathaniel. Bob was diagnosed with a degenerative eye disease at 17, and is now considered legally blind. His many other interests include coaching youth leagues, music, reading, writing, and fishing.

Rick Copus is a singer, songwriter, worship leader and ministry affiliate of Joni and Friends. Rick is the CEO of The Rick Copus Band, Inc., a non-profit music ministry that focuses on disability awareness. The band plays at special events around the country and recently released their first single and music video, *Don't Give Up on Me* (www.therickcopusband.org). Rick and his wife, Amy, live in Bakersfield, California, with their three children.

Dr. Dave Deuel is the Academic Director of The Master's Academy International, a consortium of ministry training schools worldwide, as well as the Director of International Academic Studies for Joni and Friends. Dave has served as Area Director for Joni and Friends and in board positions for the North Los Angeles Regional Center, All Children's Hospital, Direct Link for the Disabled and the Governor's Advisory committee for Disability, Sacramento, California. He is Chairman for the Old Testament and Ancient Near Eastern consultation of the Evangelical Theological Society. Dave completed an M.A. and Ph.D. from Cornell University and the University of Liverpool.

Jon Ebersole has served with Joni and Friends since 1999, and currently oversees the 23 local field ministry offices in the U.S. He and his wife have three children, two with cerebral palsy, making his 30 years of experience with disability very personal. Jon holds a Masters in Social Work from the University of Illinois and a Seminary Certificate of Biblical Studies from Trinity International University.

Dave Elsinger is a missionary with EFCA/ReachGlobal in Minneapolis, Minnesota. He and his wife, Oksana, have two children, Stephen and Elizabeth. They returned to the U.S. after six years of church planting ministry in Ukraine to get early intervention for Stephen who has autism. Dave serves missionaries by developing life-long learning tools which help them to be more fruitful in their ministry. Dave and Oksana have been blessed to travel back to Ukraine several times with their children to help educate parents and professionals about autism therapy and to share their faith in Jesus Christ.

Dr. Richard Gathro is the Director of Pepperdine University's Washington, D.C. Program and has served in higher education for more than 40 years. Rich and his wife, Kathy, and daughter, Katarina, live in Arlington, Virginia. Their son, Will, lives at Cornerstone Ranch in McKinney, Texas. This family of baseball nuts also loves the theatre, film, music and palm trees in Florida.

Michael Hoggatt is a Professor at Saddleback College in Mission Viejo, California. Michael and his wife, Mandy, are also involved with Young Life Capernaum, a ministry outreach to young adults with disabilities. Michael and Mandy live in Orange County, California, with their two children.

Will Kantz, M.A., is a counselor whose practice has included helping children with autism and their families, consulting as an in-home trainer for school districts, and speaking nationally on the impact of autism on the family. He is the co-founder of Next Things Productions, which specializes in developing music-based curriculum for children with language difficulties. Will is the proud father of two daughters and two sons.

Tim Kuck is Co-Founder of Nathaniel's Hope, a ministry dedicated to sharing hope and practical assistance to children with special needs (VIP Kids) and their families, as well as educating and equipping local churches to welcome these families. The birth of Tim's son, Nathaniel, brought their family into the special needs community and his move from Earth to Heaven launched Nathaniel's Hope. Tim is the co-owner of Regal Marine Industries where he serves as the COO and Executive Vice President. He resides in Orlando with his wife, Marie, and their two daughters.

Dr. Mark Mucklow has served as the pastor of the First Southern Baptist Church in Glendale, Arizona, since 1993. He has taught at Grand Canyon University and Golden Gate Baptist Theological Seminary as an adjunct professor. Mark serves on the boards of Southwestern Baptist Theological Seminary and Arizona Baptist Children's Services. He has served as a Chaplain in the U.S. Army Reserve. Mark and his wife, Tricia, have been married since 1988 and have four children.

215

Brent Olstad entered the world of disability in 1990 when his oldest child, Bryce, was born with spina bifida. Brent is a published music arranger and composer, the minister of music at his church in Oregon, and the volunteer Area Director of Joni and Friends Southern Oregon. He and his wife, Rachel, have three delightful children.

Earle Rice has been married for 26 years to Betty Simpson Rice. They are parents to Janelle and her husband, Cody Hudson, Nicholas and Kendall, and grandparents to Tony. Earle graduated from Kansas Wesleyan and has master's degrees from William Carey International University and Regent University. He is involved in various business activities and enjoys traveling, history, reading, walking, swimming, making music, and acting in plays. Earle participated in the Wheels for the World outreach in Trujillo, Peru, in 2007. He is presently a Chair Corps representative in Wichita, Kansas, collecting used wheelchairs and walkers to be refurbished in Kansas prisons for Wheels for the World.

Dr. A. Charles Ware is president of Crossroads Bible College and served for five years as pastor of Crossroads Bible Church. He serves on the board of the Association of Baptists for World Evangelism (ABWE) and Anchors Away. Dr. Ware is a sought-after speaker in the U.S. and abroad and also serves as a consultant on racial reconciliation. He is the author of *Prejudice and the People of God* and *How Revelation and Redemption Lead to Reconciliation*. He co-authored *One Race One Blood* and has contributed to numerous other books. He and his wife, Sharon, have been married for 39 years and have six children.

Endnotes

Foreword
1. *A Long Obedience in the Same Direction* is the title of a book by Eugene H. Peterson first published in 1980.

Chapter 1
1. See 1 Corinthians 10:13-14.
2. See www.cdc.gov/ncbddd/autism/data.html.
3. See Genesis 32:9-12.
4. Jacqui Goetz Bluethmann, "Dads Dealing with a Special Needs Diagnosis in their Kids," *Metro Parent*, http://fathersnetwork.org/wp-content/uploads/2012/10/Connec-tions-summer-2012.pdf.
5. See Psalm 139:13-14.
6. See Colossians 1:16.
7. See Psalm 46:1-2,7.
8. See 1 Samuel 20:41, 30:4; Luke 19:41-44; John 11:35.
9. See John 8:12
10. See Psalm 127:3, *NLT.*
11. See Psalm 37:4.

Chapter 2
1. See Genesis 1:27.
2. See Psalm 139:13-16.
3. See Romans 8:28.
4. W. Phillip Keller, *A Shepherd Looks at Psalm 23* (Grand Rapids, Michigan: Zondervan Publishing House, 2007), 19-20.
5. See 1 Corinthians 13:12, *The Promise; Contemporary English Version* (Nashville, Tennessee: Thomas Nelson Publishers, 1995), 1334.
6. See 2 Corinthians 12:9-10.
7. See Job 1:18-20.
8. See Job 10:1-7; 14; 18-22; 28:12; 29; 30.
9. See Matthew 6:8.
10. Larry J. Waters and Roy B. Zuck, *Why, O God? Suffering and Disability in the Bible and Church* (Wheaton, Illinois: Crossway, 2011), 122-123.
11. See Hebrews 13:5.

Chapter 3
1. See Exodus 15:26b.
2. "How He Loves" by songwriter John Mark McMillan, David Crowder lyrics, Integri-ty's Hosanna Music, http://www.metrolyrics.com/how-he-loves-lyrics-david-crowder. html.
3. Joni Eareckson Tada, "Notice the Me's," *More Precious Than Silver* (Grand Rapids, Michigan: Zondervan Publishing House, 1998), devotion for March 24.
4. See Philippians 4:6.
5. See Romans 8:15.

6. Steve Bundy, "Does My Son Need to be Healed?" *Beyond Suffering: A Christian View on Disability Ministry, Study Guide* (Agoura Hills, California, Joni and Friends, 2011).
7. See Matthew 10:8, *New American Standard Bible*
8. Bundy, *Ibid.*
9. See Mark 14:66-72, Acts 2.
10. Joni Eareckson Tada and Dave and Jan Dravecky, General Editors. *Encouragement Bible: The Answer for Those Who Hurt NIV* (Grand Rapids, Michigan, Zondervan Publishing House, 2001), 1409.

Chapter 4
1. See http://www.merriam-webster.com/dictionary.
2. See John 10:17-18.
3. James Dobson, *When God Doesn't Make Sense* (Wheaton, Illinois: Tyndale House Publishers, Inc., 1993), 61-62
4. See 1 John 1:9.
5. See www.atcp.org.
6. The documentary of Tim Borland's ultra-marathon for A-T can be viewed at: www.featmovie.com.

Chapter 5
1. "A Hero's Hero," *Connections: A Newsletter for Fathers and Families of Children with Special Needs,* Summer 2012, 5–6, http://fathersnetwork.org/wp-content/uploads/2012/10/Connections-summer-2012.pdf.
2. See Luke 17:33; Galatians 6:7; Philippians 1:21; 2 Corinthians 12:9–10; Mark 10:15; Matthew 20:26
3. See Philippians 2:1-11.
4. See Matthew 25:40.
5. See Genesis 44.
6. Henri J. M. Nouwen, *Can You Drink the Cup?* (Notre Dame, Indiana: Ave Maria, 2006), 115, 117–119.
7. See www.seeJesus.net.
8. Paul Miller, "Loving Kim," *Discipleship Journal,* no. 131 (2002): 21–26.
9. See Isaiah 11:10.
10. See Luke 7:36-50.
11. See John 13:1-17.

Chapter 6
1. Names have been changed.
2. See Ephesians 5:31–32.
3. See Malachi 2:16.
4. Daniel J. Vance. "The Effect of Children with Disabilities on Marital Stability" https://www.facebook.com/pages/Disabilities-By-Daniel-J-Vance/128993857110691. Used by permission.
5. Joni and Ken Tada, *Joni & Ken: An Untold Love Story* (Grand Rapids: Zondervan, 2013), 130.
6. *Ibid.*, pp. 137-138.
7. See http://www.joniandfriends.org/family-retreats/.
8. See Buddy Breaks at http://www.nathanielshope.org/events-programs/buddy-break/.

9. See Jill's House at www.jillshouse.org.
10. Lon Solomon, *Brokenness: How God Redeems Pain and Suffering* (Potomac, Maryland: Red Door, 2005), xv, xvii–xviii.

Chapter 7

1. See Proverbs 22:6.
2. *God's Little Instruction Book for Dad: A Collection of Simple, Humorous, and Inspirational Sayings to Quiet the Chaos of Your Busy World* (Tulsa, Oklahoma: Honor Books, 1996), 70.
3. See Psalm 139:1-4.
4. See Genesis 16.
5. See 2 Corinthians 12:10.
6. See Psalm 77:14.
7. See Ephesians 2:10.
8. See Jeremiah 29:11; Psalm 139:14.
9. See Isaiah 55:8-9.
10. See Romans 8:28.
11. See Deuteronomy 6:1-9.

Chapter 8

1. Jacquie Goetz Bluethmann, "Dads Dealing with a Special Needs Diagnosis in their Kids," *Metro Parent*, December 2011, http://www.metroparent.com/Metro-Parent/December-2011/Dads-Dealing-with-a-Special-Needs-Diagnosis-in-their-Kids/.
2. David Lyons and Linda Lyons Richardson, *Don't Waste the Pain: Learning to Grow Through Suffering* (Colorado Springs, Colorado: NavPress, 2010), 239.
3. *Ibid.*, 243.
4. See Psalm 119:11.
5. See Hebrews 4:16.
6. See Hebrews 10:23-25.
7. Dave Deuel, "Outreach and In-Reach to Families Affected by Disabilities: Ministering through Family Groups," *Beyond Suffering Study Guide* by Joni Eareckson Tada and Steve Bundy (Agoura Hills, California: Joni and Friends, 2011).
8. Shell, *Connections*, Summer 2012, 1, http://fathersnetwork.org/wp-content/uploads/2012/10/Connections-summer-2012.pdf. See also Washington State Fathers Network, www.fathersnetwork.org.
9. *Connections*, Winter 2013, 10, http://fathersnetwork.org/wp-content/uploads/2013/04/Connections-Winter-2013-Final.pdf.
10. Dietrich Bonhoeffer, *Life Together: The Classic Exploration of Faith in Community* (San Francisco, California: HarperOne, 2009). See also Goodreads, http://www.goodreads.com/quotes/688594-the-christian-however-must-bear-the-burden-of-a-brother.

Chapter 9

1. Doug Mazza, "Down with Teamwork! Creating a Christ-centered Mastermind," *Outcomes*, Summer 2012, 30-31, http://ym.christianleadershipalliance.org/?DownWithTeamwork.
2. See Matthew 18:19-20.
3. See Proverbs 27:17.
4. See Ecclesiastes 4:12.
5. See Hebrews 13:5.

6. See Proverbs 31:8.
7. Joni Eareckson Tada & Friends, *Life in the Balance: Biblical Answers for the Issues of Our Day* (Ventura, California: Regal, 2010), 195–96.

Chapter 10
1. See Romans 12:15, *ESV.*
2. Job 13:5, *NLT*
3. Jerry Bridges, *Trusting God: Even When Life Hurts* (Colorado Springs, Colorado: NavPress, 2008), preface.
4. *Ibid.*, chapter 1.
5. Lyons and Lyons Richardson, *Don't Waste the Pain.* Used by permission. All rights reserved. www.navpress.com.
6. *Ibid.*
7. "The Problem of Evil and Suffering in Our World," *Beyond Suffering Study Guide.*
8. See www.NathanielsHope.org.
9. Special Needs Alliance, http://specialneedsalliance.org.
10. World Institute on Disability, http://wid.org/center-on-economic-growth/ programs-of-the-center-on-economic-growth/access-to-assets/fact-sheets/ special-needs-or-supplemental-needs-trusts
11. Philip Yancey, *The Question That Never Goes Away* (Grand Rapids, Michigan: Zondervan, 2014).

Study Guide
1. Josh McDowell, *The Father Connection* (Nashville, Tennessee: B&H Publishing Group, 1996, rev. 2008), p. 6.
2. Rick Johnson, *Better Dads, Stronger Sons* (Grand Rapids, Michigan: Revell, 2006), p. 25.
3. Billy Graham, *Nearing Home: Life, Faith and Finishing Well* (Nashville, Tennessee: Thomas Nelson, 2011), pp. 166-167.

About the Authors

Doug Mazza, President and Chief Operating Officer of Joni and Friends, has overseen an explosive era of growth in ministry and program expansion since coming to Joni and Friends in 1999. Applying his award-winning expertise and skills in corporate leadership, after serving as senior executive for American Suzuki Motor Corporation and Hyundai Motor America, Doug has taken the vision of Joni Eareckson Tada and helped create all that Joni and Friends is today – the authoritative voice on Christian outreach to the world's one billion people with disabilities and their families. Ministering to his son, Ryan, through more than 30 years with severe disabilities, Doug Mazza brings a warm and personal perspective to the development of every program at Joni and Friends.

Steve Bundy is Vice President of the Joni and Friends Christian Institute on Disability. He was a contributing author to *Life in the Balance: Biblical Answers for the Issues of Our Day*, and co-executive producer with Joni Eareckson Tada of the Telly-Award winning television episodes, "Making Sense of Autism: Myths That Hide the Truth" and "Truth for the Church." Steve is an adjunct professor at California Baptist University and lectures on disability ministry at educational institutions and conferences around the world. He frequently appears on "Joni and Friends" television episodes and national radio, and has written articles or been interviewed for *Christianity Today, Charisma Magazine, Focus on the Family* and others. Steve and his wife Melissa know firsthand the joys and challenges of parenting a child with special needs, as their own son, Caleb, was born with a chromosome deletion which resulted in global delay and a secondary diagnosis of autism. Steve holds a B.A. in Theology and Missions and an M.A. in Organizational Leadership. He is a licensed minister and has served as a pastor and missionary.

221

Joni and Friends
Family Retreats

At both U.S. and International Family Retreats, persons with disability and their families receive encouragement and care in the comfort of a safe and accessible family camp environment. Enjoy fully-accessible and age-appropriate fun activities, be nourished by hearty home-style meals, and glean from meaningful conversations with a network of families who understand the challenges of life with disability. Short Term Missionaries (STMs) volunteer and serve families with Christ-like encouragement and friendship. Visit www.joniandfriends.org/family-retreats/ for more information and the current schedule.

and Friends
INTERNATIONAL DISABILITY CENTER

www.joniandfriends.org · P.O. Box 3333, Agoura Hills, CA 91376
(818) 707-5664 · Fax: (818) 707-2391 TTY: (818) 707-9707

Resources available from Joni and Friends

Another Kind of Courage – Video

Meet authors Doug Mazza and Steve Bundy in this introductory video and hear why they feel compelled to reach out to dads:

http://www.joniandfriends.org/anotherkindofcourage

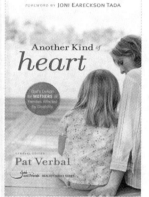

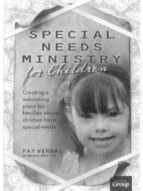

Another Kind of Heart: God's Design for Mothers of Families Affected by Disability

Pat Verbal, General Editor

When a family is affected by disability, all are affected. Fathers, mothers, sisters, brothers, extended family, even caregivers—each has their own questions and needs. The Healthy Family Series provides the support you need to be an extraordinary family to a child with special needs.

Softcover - 224 pages
Price: $14.99
Coming in 2015!

Special Needs Ministry for Children

Pat Verbal, General Editor

Are you starting or expanding a special needs ministry? This collection of case studies and practical advice will help you address the concerns of children with special needs -and their families. You'll learn to: develop and organize a program, recruit volunteers, publicize and promote the work, and more.

Softcover – 204 pages
Price: $19.00
Product Code: BK147

Joni & Ken: An Untold Love Story

By Ken and Joni Eareckson Tada, with Larry Libby

After 30 years of marriage, Ken and Joni offer readers a rare and candid account of their journey through quadriplegia, depression, pain, and cancer – and reveal a hope founded on God's grace alone. Let their story inspire and encourage your own life and marriage!

Hardcover – 192 Pages
Price: $19.00
Product Code: BK146

www.joniandfriends.org · P.O. Box 3333, Agoura Hills, CA 91376
(818) 707-5664 · Fax: (818) 707-2391 TTY: (818) 707-9707